Postcards From
A Navy Chaplain

To Joan

many good wishes
& Blessings!

Fr. Sturdy op

Postcards From
A Navy Chaplain

Reverend Joseph A. Scordo, O.P.
CDR Joseph A Scordo, CHC, USN (ret.)

Washington, DC
2016

Contents

Acknowledgements

When one has been so blessed by God as I have for my priesthood, my brothers in St. Dominic, my careers, my friends, and for life itself, it is difficult—nearly impossible—to properly express my gratitude.

That being said, I want to acknowledge just a few people who were instrumental in the publication of this little booklet. First, let me mention The Very Rev. Luke Clark, O.P., the Prior of the Dominican House of Studies in Washington, DC. A year or so ago, after having read some of the basics of this publication, he urged me to have them published. It never would have occurred to me to do so. I was simply wondering if these accounts of two of my deployments were worth archiving somewhere. His insight and enthusiasm for the project impelled me to bring these writings to a wider audience.

Allow me, also, to single out His Eminence Cardinal (then Archbishop) Edwin O'Brien, who was, during my time in the military, the Archbishop for the Military Services, USA. His unflagging support for me and for all the priests serving our young men and women in uniform was completely inspiring and even energizing.

Thanks, too, to His Excellency Archbishop Timothy Broglio who is the Ordinary for the Archdiocese for the Military Services. He faithfully accomplishes the daunting task of heading an Archdiocese caring for almost two million service men and women, their families, ambassadorial staffs, and Veteran Facilities spread all over the globe. And I would be remiss if I didn't acknowledge His Excellency Bishop Richard Higgins, who serves as one of the Auxiliary Bishops in the Archdiocese for the Military. When hearing of my work on this collection of stories, he urged me to carry it on to completion.

Next, let me thank Rev. Philip Neri Reese, O.P. Since I am a dinosaur at things computer, he helped me a great deal in getting these writings into their final form. Without his expertise, and his enthusiastic cheerleading from the side, the "Postcards" would never have been published. Thanks, as well, to Brother Jordan Zajac, O.P. whose editorial skill helped to polish these pages for publication. I extend my gratitude to Rev. Antoninus Niemiec, O.P. and especially to Rev. Innocent Smith, O.P. for their expertise. A special "thank you" goes to Graham and Lucia Summers for their help in publishing this work and building the web page.

Finally, allow me to thank and praise the brave young men and women who wear the uniform of the U.S. Armed Forces and who dedicate themselves daily to the task of defending freedom not only here at home, but also all over the world. Their bravery and devotion to duty are an inspiration to me and give me great hope for the future of this wonderful country.

Surely, I am forgetting someone in my listings here, and if I have, I offer my apology. One usually doesn't accomplish much by him or herself—with the exception, of course, of Almighty God. Thank You, Lord!

— Fr. Scordo, O.P. (March 2016)

Foreword

Father Joe Scordo's ministry of the Marines and Sailors of the 26th MEU and his support of their families before, during and after our history-making deployment to Afghanistan were crucial to the success of our mission.

By early September 2001, we had completed our training and were prepared for any contingency as our Nation's "force in constant readiness." Our Marines and Sailors and their families were anticipating a routine deployment spent honing their skills with scheduled exercises and training, occasional liberty ports, and potentially responding to any crisis that arose in the Mediterranean or the Persian Gulf while we were there. When the brutal terrorist attacks of September 11 occurred just prior to our departure, everything changed. We all understood that as the "tip of the spear", we would likely be involved in our country's immediate response to these attacks, and we would face challenges that would test our capabilities and put us in harm's way. Our Marines and Sailors and their families rose to the challenge, and all were equally committed to the successful accomplishment of our mission and the safe return of every member of the MEU.

Because of increased security, our port visits were few and very limited. As always, operational security prevented us from sharing any information with our loved ones about where we were going, when we would be there and what we would be doing. Because of the uncertainty and anticipation over what we might face, the MEU families were fearful and anxious, hungry for any information we could provide to set their minds at ease. Knowing that their families were taken care of would enable the Marines and Sailors of the MEU to focus on the tasks at hand, whatever they may be. This is where Father Joe's "Postcards" and his role as the 26th MEU Family Readiness Officer were of utmost importance, and he did not disappoint.

Father Joe's constant presence among the Marines and Sailors and his genuine concern for their well-being inspired trust and confidence; they loved and respected him. His quick response and efficient handling of emergency messages that arrived through the Red Cross, his spot-on spiritual guidance, and his continuous efforts to assist our service members and their loved ones with any issues at home that might be a distraction, had a tremendous impact on our ability to perform effectively. Father Joe's affable personality and consistently good humor helped to relieve tension, and his enthusiasm and positive attitude helped keep things in perspective when the going got tough. When we were too busy to write or call home, Father Joe did it for us, working with the Key Volunteers stateside to convey as much information as possible without compromising operational security.

Father Joe's regular "Happy Grams" as he called them, were cheerfully reassuring. In spite of the fact that we were unable to spend much time enjoying liberty, he described the beauty and cultures of the places that and people who surrounded us with the eloquence and detail of an experienced travel writer. He always focused on the good, the silver linings in any situation, never dwelling on negatives or unknowns. He showed sincere interest in every Marine and Sailor and the importance of the roles they served, highlighting the accomplishments of every shop and unit within the MEU no matter how small, and acknowledging the significance of their contributions to our success. His obvious respect and admiration for the professionalism and hard work of these men and women instilled an intense sense of pride and renewed commitment. His attention to the preparation, competence, ingenuity and resourcefulness of the troops when faced with frustrating circumstances inspired complete confidence in our capabilities. The message conveyed was, "Don't worry, we got this!"

Father Joe often shared humorous anecdotes (although many of the more colorful ones are not included here, he'd probably be happy to share them over a beer with anyone who's interested) and recalled every day incidents of interest that served to lighten the mood and evoke an appreciation for things we all take for granted back home. Regardless of the seriousness of our mission and the constant vigilance it required, we were still having fun, always missing our loved ones, and determined to return safely home to them. Likewise, the families felt empowered to handle things at home, knowing they were part of something bigger, serving their country through their sacrifices. Again, his communications created a sense of calm confidence and proud dedication to duty that were essential to our success. Father Joe's impact on the readiness and morale of the 26th MEU cannot be understated.

In re-reading "Postcards" and recalling in retrospect their importance to the overall well-being of 26th MEU during a difficult deployment, we want to further express our heartfelt gratitude, love and respect for Father Joe and his continuous efforts on behalf of our Marines and Sailors and their families.

With sincere appreciation,

Col. Andrew P. Frick, USMC (ret.)
Commanding Officer, 26th MEU(SOC)

Mrs. Jeanette Frick
Wife of Commanding Officer 26th MEU Family Readiness Advisor/Key Volunteer Coordinator

Preface: A Call To Serve

When I was preparing for my ordination to the priesthood for the Order of Preachers (Dominicans) in June of 1969, there were several options open to me for ministry as a Roman Catholic priest in our Province of St. Joseph. Since we are the Order of Preachers, the Itinerant Preaching Ministry (called back then "The Mission Band") was a possibility. However even as a young man, the prospect of "living out of a bag" was not very appealing to me. Since I was not qualified or credentialed to formally teach in a University setting, teaching was out. Then there was the possibility of becoming a foreign missionary. That ministry was *entirely* out of the question. After all, the missionary, of necessity, would have to leave home and familiar surroundings, learn a whole new language and customs, and sometimes live in austere and difficult surroundings. That certainly wasn't for me! So among all the possibilities for ministry (of which I have mentioned but a few) the one that stood out for me was the pastoral ministry of a parish priest. There it was: something I was familiar and comfortable with! There really *was* a place for me in our Province!

So I embarked for a period of parochial ministry for close to 20 years. The work was at times challenging, daunting, sometime frustrating, but above all extremely successful and satisfying. During those years I had been a Parochial Vicar, a Pastor of a parish, and a religious superior; and all of these more than once. Then, in the autumn of 1987, I was finishing up an assignment in one of our parishes and was ready to move on to yet another parish assignment. The document of assignment (a *Mandamus*, we call it) hadn't been issued, but the plans and the move were "in the works". Then one day I got a letter in a general mailing from the Navy's Chief of Chaplains Office discussing the plight of the Navy Chaplain Corps in not having enough Catholic priests to serve. The letter stated that because of the critical shortage of Catholic priests, there might be some elements of the Navy and Marine Corps (Navy Chaplains take care of Sailors, Marines, Coast Guardsmen, and even the merchant Marine) that might go six months without Mass or Sacraments. That sentence was very unsettling to me. The more I thought and prayed about it, the more I began to experience a "call" to serve in the Navy as a Chaplain. I wasn't having a mid-life crisis, and I wasn't trying to escape anything. But here was something I could do to help alleviate a need in the church and maybe even broaden my own experience. Having gotten permission from my religious superiors, I applied to the Navy, and on Christmas Eve 1987, I was notified that I was accepted for commissioning into the United States Navy!

Among all the pre-requisites that had to be met in order to be commissioned as a chaplain, there was one special one that involved a familiarization course conducted by the Archdiocese for the Military Services, USA, headquartered in Washington, DC. The course lasted several days, and included Catholic priests who currently were applying for chaplaincy in several of the services—not just the Navy. As priests and Catholic Chaplains, we fell under the religious jurisdiction of the Military Archbishop. There would be no territorial boundaries that would limit our ministry—we served literally all over the world! The talks we listened to were informative and helpful, and the priestly camaraderie was wonderful. However, there was one talk, or at least one sentence, that stood out for me and still does 28 years later. Archbishop Joseph Ryan, then the Ordinary of the Archdiocese for the Military Services, started out his address to us with: "You are all missionaries". "No", I thought! That's precisely the ministry I wanted to avoid. Yet, there it was! I was soon to discover that, indeed, I would leave familiar surroundings, learn a new language (military terms and acronyms) and a new culture, and live in sometimes difficult and arduous situations. Happily, I discovered that I could do it all. I *was* a missionary after all! In fact, I successfully carried out all different forms of ministry in the Navy Chaplain Corps. I preached half way around the world (talk about "itinerant"!), and both ashore and afloat I taught scores of military personnel preparing to convert to Catholicism in the Rite of Christian Initiation of Adults or completing their Sacraments of Initiation with Confirmation. I celebrated Mass and Sacraments in base chapels or afloat, or in the field, counseled and advised hundreds of military members, young and old alike, and I couldn't have been happier and felt more fulfilled.

I thank God constantly for the incredible gift He gave me in calling me to serve as a Navy Chaplain. On the day of my ordination I never could have imagined that this is what the Lord had planned. But his goodness and wisdom is greater than we can imagine, and I will be grateful for it forever.

***

If there are any Catholic priests or seminarians reading these pages, I most strongly and heartily recommend the ministry in the military chaplaincy, whatever the branch. There are even fewer priests today than in 1987, and the need is even more critical. You are so necessary for the spiritual life and well-being of countless men and women in uniform, and so many others. You will discover that your life and ministry will be forever enhanced. And, except for my current, more advanced age, I'd do it all over again in a heartbeat!

Introduction

As a Chaplain in the United States Navy for 20 years, I worked on the "Blue Side" (Navy) and the "Green Side" (US Marines). Navy Chaplains serve the Navy, Marine Corps, Coast Guard and Merchant Marine. In one of my last tours with the Marines, I was stationed at Camp Lejeune, North Carolina as the Chaplain for the Command Element of the 26th Marine Expeditionary Unit (26 MEU).

Among my responsibilities while deployed with the MEU was the writing of a weekly report that was emailed back to Camp Lejeune to be recorded on the MEU's "Care Line". Family and friends of the deployed men and women could call and get a short (sometimes!) message about where the MEU was, and what it was doing. Of course I had to be very careful not to divulge any information about specific exercises, locations, and operations until that information was officially released. Operational Security (OPSEC) was critically important for the safety and well-being of all the members of the MEU. By the time of the second deployment (2001–2002) email connectivity was much better. So besides sending the weekly report back home for the "Care Line", I was able to send copies to the wife of our Commanding Officer, to members of the Key Volunteers who would disseminate them to various spouses, as well as to members of my family and my friends. Lots of people were able to find out what was going on at the outset of the war in Afghanistan.

In this little booklet you will find the weekly reports of two deployments for the period 2000-2002. I first gave them then the whimsical title "HAPPY GRAMS" since they would contribute to putting at ease the minds of those family members and friends who stayed behind while their loved one deployed. However, later I changed the name for this collection to "POSTCARDS FROM A NAVY CHAPLAIN". It just seemed more appropriate. In addition to the weekly reports, you will find some stories that describe the training that the MEU goes through to be designated "Special Operations Capable" or SOC. Other items of interest are included as well. You will notice the difference in tempo and experiences for each of the deployments: pre- and post-9/11.

It is my hope that you will enjoy these little offerings and get a better idea of what goes on when a Navy/Marine Corps team deploys. And perhaps you will gain some insight into my being extremely proud of our men and women in uniform. And as the Marines say: SEMPER FI!

First Deployment
August – December 2000

Part One: Pre-9/11

In this section you will find a weekly report of our 2000 Deployment to the Mediterranean. As mentioned in the introduction, these reports were to be recorded on the MEU's CARE LINE back at Camp Lejeune. Therefore, they had to be brief accounts spelling out the locations of the ships in our Amphibious Ready Group (ARG), the activities of the MEU elements aboard USS SAIPAN, and a brief description of the port calls. You will also find expanded descriptions of our stay in Croatia as well as accounts of the training exercises conducted in preparation for the next deployment in 2001.

August 10, 2000
HELLO TARRAGONA!

Having arrived at the MEU shortly we deployed, I didn't have the opportunity to be involved in much of the intense training that is required for the MEU to be designated SOC (Special Operations Capable). A description of some of this type of training will be given at the end of this section. Before I knew it, however, I embarked aboard our ship, USS SAIPAN (LHA 2), crossed the Atlantic, stopped at the Naval Base at Rota, Spain, and sailed into the Mediterranean Sea. There was a short port call at Palma de Mallorca. And it was off again! Throughout the deployment there were several training exercises that took place. Among them were The Armed Forces Mountain School in Slovenia, Atlas Hinge in Tunisia, and Destined Glory in Turkey... plenty of training ashore for various sections of the MEU. Then there were several exercises carried out while underway. There wasn't a whole lot of "down time". Later, after yet another period of intensive training at sea, SAIPAN pulled into Tarragona, Spain. While USS AUSTIN went to Cannes, France, and USS ASHLAND put in at Palma de Mallorca.

Tarragona was a little-known port among the Sailors and Marines, but was soon to be an attractive port call for all. Tarragona was a working port for Sailors and Marines of the SAIPAN, and after a full day's work liberty call was sounded. The city is an ancient one, pre-dating the Christian era, and a very important strategic and eventual colonial city for the Romans. Consequently, the city is filled with ancient Roman ruins which were explored by the Sailors and Marines formally as members of guided tours and informally as they made their own way through the antiquities. The city's economy presently is based on the chemical industries here, but locals believe that tourism will soon be the mainstay. Our Sailors and Marines also had the opportunity for tours to the local countryside with destinations of the sources of Spanish champagne, the Monastery of Monserrat with the famed "Black Madonna" image, and an overall taste of rural and costal Spain. Some got together and arranged their own trips up to Barcelona, the site of the recent Summer Olympics. They were treated to the sights and sounds of this interesting city with its beautiful plazas and fountains, and, of course, the beautiful Cathedral of the "Sagrada Familia." All in all it was a great stop off and a good break in the intensive training that continually goes on during a "Med Float". Today, after again an intensive several days at sea filled with drills and training, we will pull into La Spezia, Italy. We look forward to a few days of relaxation in the northern Italian provinces.

August 16, 2000
LA SPEZIA VISIT

On a sunny Thursday afternoon, SAIPAN dropped anchor at La Spezia on the North West Coast of Italy, while AUSTIN pulled into Civitavechia, and ASHLAND into Livorno, all of which are Italian port cities. For SAIPAN, LaSpezia was the first non-pier side stop, and we made use of two "water taxis", fairly large boats seating about 350 each. After work each day when "liberty call" was sounded, Marines and Sailors queued up for the boat ride in to begin their Italian adventure. Having completed a pleasant 1/2 hour boat ride we reached fleet landing, an area in the "military zone." La Spezia is a fairly large Italian Naval Base and shipyard with many Italian ships home ported there. Upon leaving the gate, one could travel on foot straight up one of the main streets, now primarily a pedestrian mall, and after about 10 to 20 minutes of easy walking, you arrive at the central station with trains in all directions to famous and not-so-famous destinations. On this walk one passes a wonderful and luxuriant garden/park/boulevard area, numerous quaint little restaurants, trattorie, and pizzerie, and tons of shops. Punctuating each block of the walk were various little outdoor cafes populated by Marines and Sailors sipping Cappuccino or sampling the local birra. Numerous little shops, piazza, restaurants, and bars could also be found on any number of side streets, again patronized by US Servicemembers. For those wishing further adventure, tours were offered to Rome and Florence, and many of our folks were overwhelmed with the richness of art and history that are fairly commonplace in this part of the world. Tours, too, to the 'Cinque Terre" (region of the five cities) allowed us Americans to get a glimpse of (and sample the cuisine of) beautiful little towns hewn out of the bases and summits of steep cliffs that drop out of the sky right into the ocean. Many hopped trains to Pisa, where Marines and Sailors leaned alongside of the famous tower! One evening our personnel were dazzled by an impossible-to-describe display of fireworks, an event postponed from a previous weekend. What good fortune for us as we encountered "sensory overload" in viewing this half-hour long spectacular sky and fire show. All in all, this magnificent Italian sojourn was overwhelmingly satisfying for our people and very often one could hear spoken that wonderful phrase: "I've got to come back here with my wife."

DESTINATION CROATIA

After a short but extremely intensive training period at sea, filled with all kinds of drills and exercises, SAIPAN approached the city of Dubrovnik in Croatia, while AUSTIN headed for Split, Croatia, and ASHLAND went to Trieste, Italy. Among the Sailors and Marines aboard SAIPAN the questions circulated: Croatia? Where's that? Dubrovnik? What's that? Most aboard had never been near Croatia, but as we made our approach to Dubrovnik, we began to realize that this was no ordinary port... at least none like we had ever seen before. Passing a series of islands, with their white limestone cliffs and beautiful green canopies pierced by tall and stately cypress trées, we moored at Dubrovnik. While there was a certain "look" of a small commercial port, by and large the impression was... well, a picture postcard. Beautiful hills dotted with cream- colored buildings with orange-red roofs were almost close enough to reach out and touch. On the heights above were the rugged and beautiful mountains with scrub vegetation and rocky ascents. All the previously spoken questions on board instantly transformed into: "WOW"!! The Marines and Sailors all had their work to do, but after all duties were accomplished, "Liberty Call" was sounded. All scattered to the winds with their "Liberty Buddies". No one was allowed to leave the ship unless they were in groups of two or more. Some took advantage of tours offered and traveled to rocky island beach-picnics; some did tours to remote little villages for meals, local folk dancing shows, and Mass celebrated in village churches; and still others elected to swim and snorkel in crystal-clear Adriatic waters. However, the most common destination was the walled "Old Town" of Dubrovnik. Founded in the 7th century and walled in the 13th, Dubrovnik presented herself as truly the "pearl of the Adriatic". One approached the "Old Town" through steep city streets festooned with Oleanders in bloom, Rhododendron, Palms and, of course, the magnificent and ubiquitous cypress trees. Once inside the main gate through the Medieval Walls and battlements, one's breath was taken away. Magnificent old buildings, palaces, churches, monasteries, shops, and restaurants greeted our eyes, as we passed along the auto-free streets paved with stones worn marble-smooth by centuries of foot traffic. Each corner turned and alley-like street traversed offered again and again astounding richness of architecture and history. It was hard to believe that a scant 8 years or so before, the city was the target of a fierce period of shelling with major explosion and fire damages. The city has been almost entirely restored, and tourists from many European countries are returning by the planeload and ferry load. A walk around atop the impressive walls was quite a workout (no "Stairmaster" needed here!), and every step in the sometime seemingly endless way up was well worth it. What awaited the climber-walker was a bird's eye view of indescribable beauty. Imagine if you will, ancient churches and monasteries, timeless palaces, narrow and quaint streets and alleys, and magnificent flowering greenery and fig trees laden with their honey-sweet fruit on one's left while the rocky white cliffs and magnificent blue Adriatic peppered with gorgeous green islands appeared on your right. Dubrovnik... you are paradise! And the people... warm, congenial, always willing to help. English was spoken just about everywhere. The Marines and Sailors were able to repay a little of the natives' hospitality by volunteering to work at a local school and orphanage. Over 160 showed up for the project. This was a wonderful and generous closure to a most astounding and delightful port call. The only complaint heard here was the lack of spouse or loved one. Plans are formulating in the minds and hearts of Marines and Sailors to return; this time with their beloved. It's just too good to do it all by one's self!

August 31, 2000
TRIESTE PRESENTATION

Ah, the word "cruise". Such a misnomer! One would normally think of sun, fun, pools, lounges, the whole "Princess Lines" package. But as every Sailor and Marine knows, cruise or float means something entirely different. Mostly it's work with a few needed and pleasant breaks in between. Our latest stop in Trieste, Italy has been a mix of work and fun. Pulling into port gave us an opportunity to see such an interesting contrast. Trieste is an exceedingly busy commercial and industrial city, and has that kind of "look". However, behind the commercial look of the port stand some very beautiful green hills with a variety of buildings and architecture spread about among the green. For example, a beautiful church and bell tower sprout from atop a lush, tree-covered hill, and not very far below sit oil and petroleum storage tanks and mounds of sand and coal at unloading points. While the city has some museums and cultural centers to be visited, some of them go unseen. You see, this is truly a "working port" and will remain so, since liberty is not called away until 1600 each day. And as all of us know, that's the reality of military life. We do, however, have the opportunity to take advantage of some pretty good tours. Venice is only a couple of hours away, and the Sailors and Marines have a chance to visit that enchanting city with its many canals and beautiful bridges—big and small. An overnight trip to Salzburg, Austria is being offered wherein our folks will be able to view this wonderful old city with its museums and famous historical sites. Some are taking the bus to Aviano Air Force Base to see what's there and to visit the American Exchange there. A few COMRELS (Community Relations Projects) are planned wherein many of our Sailors and Marines will be able to do some physical labor to benefit the local community's churches and schools. But perhaps the biggest attraction has been the nightly "Beer on the Pier". Each night MWR has sponsored a tent wherein beer is sold at a buck a can, and our Sailors and Marines can get some hot dogs and sausages on a bun and just sit back with their buddies and enjoy a relaxing evening talking, laughing, and even singing to the wide variety of tunes that are being played all evening. It's been a big hit and it sure is good to see everyone having a good time without spending a whole lot of money. It looks like we will remain in Trieste longer than originally scheduled since we will be here doing regular, planned maintenance for the ship and Marine equipment. No doubt more opportunities will present themselves here to grow in our European experience while we work a lot and play a bit.

September 7, 2000
TRIESTE (PART TWO)

While USS AUSTIN and USS ASHLAND pulled into Souda Bay in Crete for a regular maintenance period, USS SAIPAN remained in Trieste for her maintenance work. The Labor Day holiday came and went quickly, and we Americans in Italy celebrated by having early liberty (at 0900) for the holiday weekend. Not everyone "vacationed", however. Elements of the Battalion Landing Team (BLT) conducted exercises at Camp Darby, an American base near Livorno, Italy.

Other members of the MEU conducted their training exercises at Camp Ederle in Vincenza, Italy. Still other members of Recon and BLT went to the Slovenian Mountain School for some training "on the rocks"—the real thing, not the drink!! For those Sailors and Marines not doing their thing at the camps and mountains, there were other opportunities afforded them. Some explored the city of Trieste more in depth, visiting churches, cathedrals, shopping malls, restaurants and pubs. Others took advantage of an overnight tour to Salzburg, Austria and were fully enveloped in that city's magic. Though Julie Andrews was not there running through the streets singing her heart out with several children following, our Sailors and Marines were able to see that wonderful city with its parks, fountains, vistas (remember, it sits at the base of the Alps) and even the Church where the famous wedding scene was shot for "The Sound of Music." The majority of our folks, however, hopped a train for a short two-hour ride to Venice. Ah Venice, for so many centuries the center of culture, art, and business for the entire Adriatic, and, in fact, the gateway to the East. Remember Marco Polo? He walked those streets! Sitting atop a cluster of islands off the Italian coast, Venice enchants the visitor with a host of canals, goldole, water taxis and busses, churches, museums, piazze—little squares here and there, and a myriad of little shops selling everything from expensive and inexpensive works of art in glass, to various leather goods, masks, and a host of other such items. And to the surprise and chagrin of many: MICKEY DEES—the ubiquitous golden arches! And who could visit Venice without stopping at St. Mark's square to view the magnificent basilica and bell tower, and be covered—literally—by pigeons looking for a "handout"? Soon, however, we bid Trieste a fond farewell, and shoved off to more work (and sometimes a little play) on our "Med 2000" sojourn.

September 14, 2000
TOTALLY TUNISIA (ALMOST)!!

On Saturday last, SAIPAN bid a fond "arrivederci" to Trieste, but not before the "Warlords" of Battalion Landing Team (BLT) 2/2 sponsored our own version of the Summer Olympics. At the closing award ceremonies (sorry; no triple-tiered winners' stand, flag raising and national anthems) the victors of the various events were announced and honored. Our Marines and Sailors participated in events such as wrestling, basketball, flag football, weightlifting, horseshoes, footraces, etc. Perhaps one of the most interesting events was the fishing contest. The top runners-up in this event brought in a mighty total of three, or four, or five fish each. However, the gold medalist, one of the mighty "Warlords", landed a total of about 24 of our finned friends. This was a catch of "biblical proportions" considering that we were pier side the whole time! Most of our work and focus this week, however, was on the joint exercises and training with the Armed Forces of Tunisia. A non-stop series of planning conferences, rehearsals, briefings, and more planning conferences took place in preparation for the exercises that are presently kicking off as you are listening to this message. Our Amphibious Ready Group's (ARG's) three ships are together again, and our Marines and Sailors are once again honing the skills that make them "a force in readiness" for freedom and security in this part of the world. All family and friends of these brave, strong, young men and women can be rightly proud of the magnificent and professional efforts and accomplishments of our Navy-Marine Corps team. There is nothing else like it in the entire world!

September 21, 2000
TUNISIAN TRIUMPH

Ah! White sands and strong sun!! This was Tunisia in North Africa this past week. However, there were no beach umbrellas, blankets and coolers for our Marines and Sailors as they went ashore to carry out and successfully complete our exercises with the Tunisian Armed Forces. As SAIPAN's landing craft (LCUs) transported troops and materiel ashore and the Marines' helicopters did the same, all were primed and ready to conquer any and every planned obstacle that stood in the way of total victory for the "forces of freedom and right." And after a couple of days of hard work by members of the MEU's Command Element, BLT (Battalion Landing Team), MSSG (MEU Services Support Group) and the ACE (Air Combat Element), our troops moved right into period of cross training with the Tunisian Military on shore. Our troops would eventually bring back interesting tales of the Tunisian troops, curious civilians, rugged terrain, and even donkeys to enlighten and entertain us all. But the blistering countryside wasn't the only site for training. Members of all elements of the Tunisian military forces came aboard our ships and had some valuable training with us afloat on the "briny deep". And at the end of it all, our troops returned, tired and sun baked, but smiling all! It was good for all of us to be back together again. The average American can hardly imagine the pride we have in ourselves and each other and the strong professional and even a kind of familial bond that forms when we are deployed. Our allies sit back in awe as they see the strength and professionalism of our Navy-Marine Corps team. The ARG (Amphibious Ready Group) then weighed anchor and started out for our next planned exercise, eager and pleased to be America's young, strong, and competent ambassadors to the Mediterranean area.

September 28, 2000
"LOCATION! LOCATION! LOCATION!"

Life goes on as usual here on the Med 2000 deployment of our Amphibious Ready Group (ARG). Having left Tunisia, we steamed on and went our separate ways in our normal, planned activities. The AUSTIN with its crew of Sailors and Marines steamed up to Croatia to participate in a joint exercise and training session with the Croatian military. The event, called CROATIAN PHIBLEX 2000, took place in the vicinity of Split, Croatia and featured landings and maneuvers ashore there. Meantime, the SAIPAN and ASHLAND continued on with the normal course of training aboard ship and planning for normally scheduled exercises that comprise the majority of our time here on deployment. Yes, Virginia, the Marines and Sailors really do work on deployment—it's not all port calls! Folks who visit our ships from time to time from so many varied stops on our deployment are consistently amazed at how well and effectively our life goes on aboard ship despite some real, and sometimes arduous living conditions. We live, eat, sleep, work and recreate in really close quarters. Despite the stresses that normally arise from such close living, the Navy-Marine Corps team develops a strong working relationship and powerful camaraderie that enables us to continue to build an extremely forceful team for fostering peace and goodwill in this part of the world. Our visitors always leave us with a new and awe-filled appreciation of the young men and women of our Navy and Marine Corps...none better in the whole wide world!

October 5, 2000
"FILL-ER-UP!"

The Marines of the 26th MEU continue their day-to-day routine of work, meetings, classes, and just living the life of being "underway". One might wonder, however, just how the ship and aircraft keep running and people get supplied with the necessities of life when we are away from land for extended periods of time. The answer is simple, but not the operation: It's called the RAS or Replenishment at Sea—another term being UNREP or Underway Replenishment. Basically what happens is this: We pull alongside a supply ship and fuel and materiel is transferred over. That sounds fairly simple, but in reality it is a complex evolution requiring an immense amount of skill and hard work. First off, the two ships must travel at a close quarters on exactly the same course at exactly the same speed—no easy feat for two large vessels. Cables are then crossed over between the ships and fuel hoses are hooked up between the two ships for the filling of our fuel tanks. At the same time there are other cables set up for CONREPS, which is Connected Replenishments. Pallets of supplies are passed over on these cables to our ship. There may even be VERTREPS, Vertical Replenishments, going on wherein helicopters pick up pallets of supplies in large, netted slings and move them from ship to ship. It is an amazing ballet of man and machinery that satisfies the needs of a large ship like SAIPAN while underway. When this complex maneuver is completed, the work is not finished. The supplies have to be moved from the cavernous hanger deck to the various storage places on board. A human chain of Marines and Sailors is formed and each box, or bundle, or package is passed person to person until it arrives at its storage destination. Remember the "bucket brigades" in the old movies, passing water from person to person to fight a fire? Well, here it's not water, it's food and supplies. This phenomenal combination of physical, mental, and mechanical strength and know-how all add up to allowing us to continue to remain the powerful Navy-Marine Corps team in the Mediterranean that is the pride of the American people. Sailors and Marines: take a bow; you deserve it!

October 12, 2000
"TABLE FOR TWO... THOUSAND!!"

Most everyone has had the experience of waiting in line for a table at a restaurant, even with reservations. Imagine if over 2,500 people showed up at one time!!! That's why aboard SAIPAN we have gone to "continuous feeding". That means we serve "chow" virtually all day long. For example: Breakfast from 6 to 10 A.M.; Lunch from 10 A.M. to 3 P.M.; and Dinner from 3 to 6:30 P.M., and that doesn't include "Midrats" (Midnight Rations), a meal for those who missed the evening meal because of standing watch. While the lines of Sailors and Marines may be a little long for meals, at least they don't stretch "from here to eternity". And the menu: "Oh MY!" How about a 35-day cycle of different entrées (and vegetables) with selections of varieties of beef, pork, fish, or poultry? Throw in a well-stocked salad bar, a wonderful dessert and pastry bar with at least 14 variations each, as well as special food events such as a potato bar or wings and the like, and you begin to get the picture. Not bad... we are proud of that, and rightly so. But how does this get accomplished? Well, on the enlisted "mess decks" alone there are at least 3 shifts of about 12 Sailors and Marines each cooking and serving the meals each day. The bakers (another couple of crews) are working round the clock to keep us supplied with flavorful breads and pastries...ever pass a bakery and catch a whiff of that wonderful bakery smell?...And then the "mess decks" have to be cleaned—tables washed down, decks swabbed, and table supplies renewed and refilled. Lots of work going on here, folks! For those of you who like facts and figures, get a load of these: over 358 thousand meals served thus far on the deployment; 7 thousand gallons of milk consumed; over 8 thousand pounds of hamburger used (look out McDonald's—here we come!) and almost 20 thousand dozen eggs served! All of this is understandable to satisfy the nutritional needs of healthy young Sailors and Marines on duty "in the Med". A tip o' the hat to the Navy-Marine Corps team that makes all of this happen each and every day!

October 19, 2000
PUSHING ON!

While America grieved because of the tragic loss of lives of our Sailors on the USS COLE, our Sailors and Marines here in the Med joined their minds, hearts and prayers to those of the families of the fallen. Various observances of public and private prayer were held here along with a wreath laying from one of the ships of the Amphibious Ready Group (ARG). But the COLE bombing would not and could not deter the Sailors and Marines of Med Float 2000 from continuing their mission of training and exercises, insuring that America still has a force of readiness for peace and security in this part of the world. USS AUSTIN and USS ASHLAND moved over to Doganbey, Turkey to begin participation in a multi-force, multi-national exercise called Destined Glory 2000. After a few days of being at sea elsewhere, USS SAIPAN joined AUSTIN AND ASHLAND. Destined Glory is a huge exercise that actually takes place not only in Turkey, but also in Greece, and in the Aegean and Eastern Mediterranean Seas, and involves maritime, air, and amphibious forces from Greece, Italy, the Netherlands, Spain, Turkey, Germany, the United Kingdom, and the United States. It goes without saying that an exercise as big as this, with a complex assortment of some 70 ships, 130 aircraft including some 60 helicopters, and over 21 thousand multi-national Soldiers, Sailors, and Marines, takes an immense effort of planning, organizing, and rehearsing to bring about the successful and safe completion of all planned exercises. Imagine, if you will, all these nations with their equipment and personnel all working together to accomplish military objectives that include joint deployments, integrated communications, and amphibious land, sea, and air activity. Lots of "inspiration and perspiration" are experienced each day by our leadership and troops so that all activities are carried out safely and successfully. Our Sailors and Marines of this Mediterranean Deployment in this way continue to be for America "A Certain Force in an Uncertain World."

October 26, 2000

EXERCISE! EXERCISE! EXERCISE!

Chalk another one up for our Navy-Marine Corps team! At this time last week, the personnel of our Med Deployment 2000 were getting into full swing with the multi-national exercise, DESTINED GLORY. Actually, the whole thing began more than a week ago with ships and forces of such countries as Turkey, Spain, Italy, Great Britain, Greece, and some other countries all coming together in an ambitious and challenging set of training exercises in Turkey. AUSTIN and ASHLAND first went to Saros Bay in Turkey to start off, and later moved down to Doganbey, Turkey to join the SAIPAN team to carry on and complete all the maneuvers and operations. Our SAIPAN folks shoved off in LCUs (landing crafts) and helicopters to the strains of "Anchors Aweigh" and "The Marine Corps Hymn", and conducted the amphibious assault landing. This was followed by a complete package of tactical training ashore. Just about the entire MEU was involved in this week-long event. Each group of artillery, tanks, LAVs (Light Armored Vehicles), helicopters, jets, recon folks, radiomen, infantry, and every other part of the MEU had their training and exercise objectives, and each carried them out to a successful conclusion. There were other periods of joint training and drills with the Turkish, Greek, and Spanish forces. And every group had a great opportunity to show the other the fine points of tactics, weapons, and safety and security measures to mention just a few. Such multi-national events give all of us an opportunity to cooperate with and learn from each other. Our Marines and Sailors returned to the ship with further sharpened skills at their jobs as well as a new awareness of just how small our planet is and how it is so necessary for all of us to be working together to maintain peace and tranquility in our world. Well done, Sailors and Marines!

November 2, 2000

THE MALTA EXPERIENCE!

While AUSTIN and ASHLAND headed for ports in Southern Italy, SAIPAN pulled into the Island nation of Malta. Malta is the largest of several islands in the Malta Archipelago, while two other smaller islands, Gozo and Comino, have several small towns and settlements. There are about three other islands in the group that are completely uninhabited. We docked in the principal and Capital city of Valletta, which has an elongated and deep natural harbor. As we approached our pier we were struck with a view of an almost Medieval City poised behind powerful and mighty walls and battlements. The city is built on solid rock and the buildings and some of the walls are constructed with the same sand-colored stone. Church domes and towers, along with buildings that almost resembled palaces, were everywhere. What a beautiful sight! The only thing that gave a hint that we were not back in the 15th and 16th centuries were the ubiquitous TV antennae. I guess they don't have cable yet!! Malta is steeped in history as old as time itself and the island has been inhabited by peoples dating back to the Phoenicians and even before! Of course, the island is mostly known for the Knights of Malta. Originally the Hospitalar Knights of St. John were founded to care for the sick and injured in the Holy Land. Over the years they were forced out of first the Holy Land, then the Greek island of Rhodes. Finally, Charles V, the Holy Roman Emperor, gave them Malta as their home with a few stipulations and a yearly rent of...yes, you guessed it...a Maltese Falcon!! Move over "Bogie"!! The Sailors and Marines were able to take advantage of many tours that were offered and quickly became aware of the heavy burdens that the Maltese people have had to endure over the centuries and the impressive and even at times convoluted history of the rulers and culture of the place. Americans become more and more aware of just how short our own history is and how fortunate we are at not having had to endure trials such as many older societies have. Traversing the narrow streets up and down steep hills one runs into castles, churches, forts, little squares, and yes, McDonalds...along with Burger King, and even Kentucky Fried Chicken! Our Sailors and Marines also had the opportunity to take part in a COMREL (community relation project) on the sister island of Gozo. There they painted and tidied up places such as orphanages, respite homes for the handicapped, and community centers. It was an act of generosity that made our Sailors and Marines again wonderful ambassadors of the United States in this area of the world. After some work and some fun, we set sail for new adventures. And once again the familiar sentence was heard from all quarters: "I'd like to come back here with my wife"!!

November 8, 2000

WE PLAY...WE WORK!

SAIPAN pulled into Naples, while AUSTIN and ASHLAND visited Malta and Sicily. Ah Naples! There's a phrase sometimes heard in America which may or may not have originated in Naples, but it goes like this: "See Naples and die!" One interpretation may very well be the one that indicates that if you see Naples, you can then die because there is nothing else in the world to look at after this wonderful city. One of the Neapolitans herself opined, however, that it might mean that if you go to Naples, you just might get hit by a car and die in its helter-skelter traffic! Whatever the true meaning, Naples was unforgettable. Naples is a busy port, (the second largest in Italy after Genoa) with all sizes of commercial and tourist ships constantly slipping in and out of the wide and scenic harbor. Some of the ever-moving ferry boats, for example, looked lumbering and clumsy, while others were sleek and almost "supersonic" in their appearance. These ferries run to not only the neighboring islands and ports, but to some fairly distant destinations up and down the Italian peninsula and even other European countries. Our Sailors and Marines had the opportunity to go on some wonderful tours, such as the all-day exploration of the ancient city of

Pompeii, buried in the first century A.D. in a cataclysmic eruption of the nearby volcano, Mt. Vesuvius, and then a climb clear up to the top of the volcano. And climb they did! Others went on trips to places like nearby Sorrento to sample the charm of that quaint vacation spot, or to Rome to be overwhelmed by the majesty and beauty of such sights as the Coliseum, the Vatican City complex with St. Peter's Basilica, and the Sistine Chapel, the Spanish Steps, the Roman Forum and many other famous Roman wonders. And our folks got a chance to experience the Roman traffic, which was almost as perilous as the Neapolitan archetype! And, of course, some chose to explore the streets of Naples itself, partaking of the local shopping and, naturally, cuisine. What a great couple of days for the 26th MEU and crew of SAPAN! Now we have moved on and shortly we will begin a two-week exercise and training period in the Croatian Military Camp located in the mountains near Slunj and nearby environs. This type of training exercise will be another "first" for 26 MEU, and we are looking forward to meeting and training with the Croatian military forces. Because we will be "in the field" we won't have the wonderful luxury of easy communication home by phone and e-mail. So in case any of the families of our Sailors and Marines don't hear from them for a week or two, please don't worry. We're all fine; it's that the field is not the boat, just as the boat is not like Camp Lejeune. But "not to worry", we will be back in touch before you know it! It's one of those sacrifices that our generous and hardy Sailors and Marines make to be at the ready should America call. And let's also not forget November 10th... *HAPPY BIRTHDAY, MARINES!*

November 11, 2000
CLIMB EVERY MOUNTAIN

Once again, Croatia surprised all the Sailors and Marines aboard SAIPAN, AUSTIN, and ASHLAND. It was hard to imagine that our experience of Dubrovnik several weeks ago would be equaled let alone surpassed, but sure enough it was. Last week the three ships pulled into the port city of Rijeka to begin the offload of people and machines for the start of Operation "Slunj 2000". Rijeka is a picturesque little port with the mandatory commercial aspects and quite a scenic view as well. Perched on steep slopes that rise immediately from the water were rather graceful high-rise apartment buildings along with two and three story, cream colored, and red roof-tiled buildings. The green hills, peppered with white limestone outcroppings, made a wonderful background for the man-made structures clearly visible even from a few miles away from the piers.

Just about all of our equipment and personnel were offloaded in about two days and transported a distance of about five hours away in the distant and mountainous central area of the country. It all went without a hitch. Our road journey began with a steep climb up the lovely coastal range of mountains, and continued ever higher through the higher elevations in the interior. We had thought that we missed the fall foliage of the States, but to our surprise there the colors were—beautiful shades of reds, browns, and yellows—and in a sense we were back in western Virginia, West Virginia, and even New England! As we reached even higher altitudes we would pass through lovely little villages with magnificent small rivers and waterfalls that babbled and meandered right through the centers of each town. It was truly a breathtaking trip. The main body arrived at the Mountain Training Area of Slunj while detachments of the Air Combat Element positioned themselves at air strips located at Udbina and KRK. Stepping off our vehicles we paused for a moment or two to look about and be taken in by the magnificent scenery. "Gorgeous" is the first word that comes to mind. The advance party had done a great job in preparing the tents and barracks that would be our work and living spaces for the next two weeks or so. Everyone hopped right to it, and in a blink of the eye, the camp and all equipment was up and running at a steady hum. Our second night there saw our final celebration of the Marine Corps Birthday when we shared a delicious roasted pig and chicken dinner with all the fixings. *WOW!* Our living accommodations were surprisingly more than adequate, more than most had expected. A large number of Sailors and Marines were housed in barracks out of the elements—not that the elements were hostile. It's been a week of record high temperatures and sunny skies. The locals told us that by now there are usually several feet of snow on the ground. Actually it felt like mid-September!

The entire MEU and all its moving parts were fully operational in just a day or so, and the training in the mountains began. If it could move, it moved; if it could shoot, it shot; and all the Marines and Sailors "did their thing"! We did some joint training with members of the Croatian military, and we hosted several Distinguished Visitor tours and observers. More VIPs are expected before we are finished. Everyone's spirits are high, and all the exercises and training "packages" are going especially well. Not only has this been a valuable and profitable training time for our Navy Marine Corps team, but it is a "huge" event for the people of Croatia. They have welcomed us with open arms and can't do enough for us. "Slunj 2000" is shaping up to be one of the 26th MEU's premier training exercises on this "Millennium Cruise, 2000".

November 16, 2000
"HOME ON THE RANGE" or "LIONS, AND TIGERS, AND BEARS, OH MY!"

Week two of "Operation Slunj 2000" proved to be a busy and soggy one. About Friday, the weather changed. It got a bit cooler and the rains came... just about every day...sometimes periodically, sometimes steadily all day. But it certainly didn't dampen the spirits or the resolve of all the elements of 26 MEU. Every unit at every level continued on with their exercises whether it was a squad, or a platoon, or company. Day and night out on the "Range", as the Croatian military calls the training area, there were live fire exercises with artillery and tanks, as well as shooting with every and all types of weapons that our Marines and Sailors are trained to use. It was a time marked by extensive troop and vehicle movements, training exercises, and even foot patrols all expertly and successfully orchestrated by extremely competent people in leadership positions at all levels. "Don't feed the bears" was one of the warnings that was given before we arrived at the training area. Since it was a mountainous and fairly wild area, bears were expected to be there. However, nary a one was sighted during our exercises. There was only one report of a sighting, but at this moment it is considered spurious. So the Davy Crockets among the Marines and Sailors were quite disappointed, to say the least, that they couldn't "bag" themselves a "bar"!! We had several distinguished visitors with us on a succession of days. General Jones, the Commandant of the Marine Corps, visited and spoke to the troops, meritoriously promoted one Marine, re-enlisted a few others, and generally proceeded around to many of the training areas to be with the Marines and Sailors. The Commanding General of II MEF (Marine Expeditionary Force) also arrived and was with us for a two-day period. He also moved around the rather extensive training area to observe the exercises and visit the troops. Sunday saw a bit of a break in the "action" for a few hours as many of the Marines and Sailors had an opportunity to go into the town of Slunj for church services. Croatia is predominantly Roman Catholic, and the Catholic Pastor invited the members of the 26th MEU to join his congregation in the celebration of Mass in town. A busload of Marines and Sailors arrived at the church along with the General, the Colonel, and many other high-ranking military and civilian officials. Catholic or not, all were warmly greeted and welcomed and the service began. The Mass was conducted completely in the Croatian language with brief interspersions in English by the 26 MEU Chaplain, himself a Catholic priest and a concelebrant at the Mass. At the end of the service sentiments of welcome and thanks were exchanged by the two priests, followed by exuberant applause and warm smiles and laughter. The locals then treated everyone to trays and trays of exquisite, home-made, local and national pastries along with cups of wonderful, strong, black coffee. What a feast! The Officers, the Mayor and other civil officials, the Marines and Sailors, the media, and the locals all mingled, smiled, ate, and genuinely enjoyed their brief but unforgettable time together. After the service, all returned to the "Range" to continue on with and complete the exercises. Most of the personnel started the return trip back to the ships at the port of Rijeka on Monday and Tuesday with the majority of equipment back by Wednesday. The rear party will arrive by the end of the week and off we go, back underway! Now that the exercises are completed, our Marines and Sailors once again direct their thoughts to home and family especially at the beginning of the holiday season. Colonel Glueck and all the members of 26 MEU send our love and warmest wishes and greetings for a wonderful Thanksgiving Day.

ON AND ON

Thanksgiving Day came and went for members of the 26th MEU. It was a day almost like any other day for us. We were still in the Croatian port of Rijeka last Thursday "back loading" the remainder of our personnel and equipment that returned from the mountain campsites of Slunj, Udbina, and KRK. Since that operation took most of the day, it was decided that we would celebrate Thanksgiving on Saturday in order to have a bit of a more leisurely "holiday." We were underway on Friday, and when Saturday came, celebrate we did! We had a relaxed schedule and we had a most magnificent holiday meal with all the trimmings. In several of the dining areas, holiday music was playing in the background, and one could easily imagine Santa arriving at the end of the Thanksgiving Day Parade in New York. The weather was beginning to turn a bit sour, but that didn't bother us much because a port visit was in the offing in just a few days. AUSTIN and ASHLAND pulled into Dubrovnik and Split in Croatia, and SAIPAN was scheduled to pull into the small Italian port city of Brindisi. But as fate would have it, that was not to happen. The foul weather turned really foul, and we experienced high winds and heavy seas. SAIPAN was "rocking and rolling" out there on the Adriatic, and from the safety of the interior of the ship we could see a very angry sea with huge swells, wind whipped whitecaps, and cloudy, rainy skies. In such conditions it is unwise for any ship, big or small, to attempt to put into port except in emergency situations, so we waited to ride out the storm. We had plenty to do, anyway. Well, the sea state stayed ugly for a couple of days, and the line handlers in the port were unable to do their work because of the high winds. So our port call was cancelled. Out here one gets a good idea of the awesome power of the forces of nature, and as big a ship as we are, we are still just a speck on the mighty seas. It's not as if the Marines and Sailors of the 26th MEU had nothing to do. We have spent a lot of time cleaning and inventorying section and personal gear, writing reports, and planning for the events to come in the next three weeks. The time passes quickly because we are busy, and now we find ourselves at the end of November! If December is here, then "you-know-what" is not far away! No wonder you see broader smiles each day on the faces of our "Blue-Green", Navy-Marine Corps team of Millennium Cruise 2000!

"GO WEST, YOUNG MAN [AND WOMAN]"

On Friday last, very early in the morning, SAIPAN (followed by AUSTIN and ASHLAND) left the Adriatic to begin the final leg of traversing the "Med." But wouldn't you know it?! The last day or so of SAIPAN's time in the Adriatic was marked by radically calming seas, a rapid dying of wind, and an eventual sea state as flat as a pond! There went our port call in Brindisi (no time now), but at that point nobody much cared. We steamed westward at a pretty good clip, passing southern Italy and Sicily. Though it was night, we could tell by the faint lights on the horizon. As is usual at sea, we didn't see much after that for a day or so, except for some sunsets that we sailed into and brilliantly illuminated the skies and clouds. Sometime on Sunday afternoon we could make out the mountains of what we knew to be Spain! The excitement level went up a notch! Then a little after midnight we passed through the Straits of Gibraltar. It had been a spectacular view in the day as we passed into the Med five months ago, but this nighttime view was magical! As we proceeded through, on our right was Europe and the populated areas around "the Rock". While the areas around the base of the great natural wonder were well lighted, the rock itself had relatively few lights on it...seven in all if memory serves. On our left was Africa and Morocco. Here and there a small city or town was lighted up, but between them were lights, presumably illuminating roadways, that resembled shimmering strings of pearls with a magnificent reddish-gold hue. Add to this scene a great deal of photo luminescent bacteria in the water that made the waves below us sparkle and glow with gorgeous blue-green light, and you had an experience that Disney probably couldn't match! Everyone also knew that as long as Spain was on our right, and Africa was on our left, we were heading in the right direction! We arrived at Rota, Spain (on the Atlantic!) Monday morning, and the Marine Corps equipment was all "offloaded" on the pier and surrounding areas for a thorough washdown with high pressure hoses, etc. You see, every vehicle or piece of equipment that touched down on foreign soil had to be thoroughly scrubbed and then inspected to ensure that we didn't bring back to the States any type of animal or bacterial life no matter how minute or harmless it might appear. The Marines worked round the clock in washing the tanks, trucks, artillery pieces, "hummers"—anything that left the ship in the past five months. Spirits were cheerful and positive, despite the long hours, because the Marines and Sailors knew that this meant that we are really close to heading back "home." As you walked along the pier, you could almost feel the excitement in the air amidst the busyness. Each day "Liberty Call" was sounded after regular working hours, and the Marines and Sailors headed off to the main Base Exchange and little eateries. Some ventured out into the beautiful little town of Rota, but since it was pretty dark pretty early, they were not able to get a wide-eyed view of the Southwestern Spanish countryside. No matter, though.

In a day or so, we will point our ships westward and happily and fondly bid Europe "Farewell" and put out into the Atlantic to head for home, our loved ones, and, of course, Santa!

"THE RAIN IN SPAIN..."

Somebody should have told Liza Doolittle of "My Fair Lady" that the plain is not the only place where the rain in Spain mainly stays! As soon as we pulled into Rota to begin our "washdown" and inspection of equipment, it began to rain...sometimes a little drizzle, sometimes downpours! But that didn't dampen the spirits of the members of 26 MEU as they set about to complete their tasks of thorough cleaning...they were wet anyway! The job was done well and quickly, and soon 26 MEU's equipment and personnel were loaded back on SAIPAN, AUSTIN, and ASHLAND, and off we sailed westward and homeward bound! Funny thing: As soon as we pulled away from the pier, the clouds broke, and the sun came shining through...just our luck!! But who cared? We were on our way home. The word "Secure for Sea" was passed, and we knew that we were in for a bumpy ride! There was a horrendous storm in the North Atlantic that played havoc with shipping, and even though we were hundreds of miles away, we would feel the effects. Did we ever! "Stand by for heavy rolls" was announced, and we soon encountered huge ocean swells under bright and clear skies. We rocked and rolled, really *ROCKED AND ROLLED*, for days. Watching folks walking to and fro in the passageways at odd angles reminded some of an amusement park "Fun House" with the tilted rooms. We tied everything down that could be tied down, but occasionally there were a few victims of the constant rolling of the ship. There were flying saucers (no aliens, however), flying tables and chairs, and occasionally a few flying persons! Through it all most people were smiling and seemed to be having a good time. It was that "Westward Bound Thing" again! Marines and Sailors were busy cleaning equipment and living and working spaces, writing reports, and packing away stuff for our North Carolina arrival. We had a Video Teleconference with the Leadership of the MEU that was on its way to take our place in the "Med." Information concerning the deployment, lessons learned, and recommendations were sent electronically, and each group was able to see the other. It wasn't hard to guess why *WE* were smiling a whole lot more than the other guys during the Teleconference! There was still a lot to do on board the ship, and we also had an opportunity to attend "Return and Reunion" briefs conducted by members of Norfolk's Family Service Center. These folks were flown out to us to help us get ready for our return and offered briefs such as "Return to Intimacy", "Singles Homeward Bound", "Returning to Children", "Highway Safety", "Buyer Beware—Car Buying", and other such topics. There was even a "shower" for new dads whose babies were born while they were on "float". So now we continue to work and wait. "Six days and a wake up",

"Five days and wake up" are phrases often heard around the ship. The smiles are getting broader, and here and there you can hear humming: "I'll Be Home for Christmas." And what a Christmas it will be! Like little kids, we can hardly wait!

December 19, 2000
THE LAST HURAH or THE FIRST HOORAY!

After bouncing around the Atlantic for several days after leaving Rota homeward bound, the seas calmed and we all breathed a sigh of relief. "The worst is over" we thought, as we set about getting the final preparations for our "offload" at Moorhead City, North Carolina and heading to Camp Lejeune when we touched American soil. But Mother Nature had some other ideas in mind! We were told to increase our speed so that we could arrive a day earlier than originally expected... apparently there was some severe weather on the way and it would be better for us to get home ahead of the storm. Now the arrival date was set for Monday the 18th of December! Smiles everywhere!! But the smiles soon faded as we encountered increasingly heavy seas and unpleasant weather as we sailed westward. "Here we go again", we thought as we started to rock and roll once again. But this time it was different: huge waves crashing against the ship and really strong winds buffeted us quite a bit. It didn't help that some had seen "The Perfect Storm" just before deploying in July! Now add variable number two: A ship was in trouble somewhere off the coast of Virginia, and we were directed to go north to aid in the rescue the crewmembers of the stricken vessel. We got half way there and were directed to turn around and resume our course towards North Carolina—the crew had been rescued and the ship had gone down. O.K., now we re-aligned all schedules for the later arrival time on Monday. Now the word was a late evening (9 P.M.) arrival, but we moved along very well, because the winds had died down and the seas flattened out. Now we were going to be earlier than the projected later arrival. Anyone who is remotely connected with the military knows that one has to be more than "flexible". It's better to be "liquid" and even sometimes "gaseous"! We also felt sorry for the welcoming committee because they, too, had to change their timeline just as we did.

Sure enough, we arrived off the shores of North Carolina and Moorehead City a couple of hours later than first expected. Vehicles and people moved away from the ship towards the shore on LCUs, the ship's landing craft. The ride was wonderful! We would be home shortly. And Mother Nature relented and apologized by presenting the most beautiful sunset of the entire cruise. We landed, we hopped on busses, and by 7 P.M. we arrived at Camp Lejeune. We were greeted by excited adults and children alike, and after lots of hugs and kisses, we were treated to pizza, cookies, sweets, and soft drinks. Ribbons hung everywhere, and balloons took their places in offices, hallways, conference room (where we consumed the welcome food), and these bright, Helium-filled adornments gave a special touch and pleasant surprise to all the returning Marines and Sailors. We were home, we were celebrating, and we were glad!

Now we can look back at the past 5 and one-quarter months and wonder: how did we get all that we did do, accomplished? In some ways it went by so quickly. We made lots of memories on this "float", memories that will keep many of 26 MEU's Sailors and Marines smiling for quite some time. And now Santa is loading up his sleigh, and we all have visions of dancing sugarplums. It's a most wonderful time of the year! And all of us here at 26th MEU wish all our readers a most happy and blessed holiday season. Come on Santa, bring it on!!!!

December 18, 2000
EVENING PRAYER AT SEA

Each evening at 2200 (10:00 PM) while underway, one of the Chaplains offers the evening prayer for the whole ship. The following was part of a joint prayer offered by the ship's chaplain and me the night before we disembarked at Moorehead City, NC.

Dear God;

'Twas the night before Moorehead and all through the boat
Some folks stood around with a lump in their throat.
Their joy and excitement running all through their veins
For just a few hours are all that remains.

We're poised for reunions with family and friend
It's hard to believe we have come to an end.
To and fro people scurry with an increasing pace
And you can't help but notice the smile on their face.

We're headed for home and the Christmas tree bright
Or it's Ramadan, Quanza, or the Chanukah light.
We're all celebrating these great gifts from You
That You care for us always is certainly true.

The mem'ries of ops won't fade very soon
Atlas Hinge, Destined Glory, and Croatia and Slunj.
We prepared, we rehearsed, we really did plan
And we all had our part, every woman and man.

And it's hard to decide which port call we liked best
Tarragona or Palma, Dubrovnik, Trieste.

There was Malta, LaSpezia, and Naples to boot.
And the washdown at Rota was really a hoot.

Through it all You were there, we know it is true
More than "Liberty Buddies", our best friend was You.
So we thank You, dear Lord, for the love that You give.
May we always be grateful as long as we live.

We're Marines and we're Sailors, One Team and One Fight
We think of it all as we wait through the night.
And we say as the shores of our home come in sight
Merry Christmas to all, and to all a good night!

CDR (Sel) Joseph A. Scordo
26 MEU (SOC) Chaplain

AN AMERICAN CATHOLIC CHAPLAIN LOOKS AT CROATIA
By LCDR Joseph A Scordo, CHC, USNR

Before deploying with the 26th Marine Expeditionary Unit (26 MEU), I must admit that I was not very familiar with the history, geography, and culture of the Balkan countries. There were several short briefings for all personnel of the MEU to familiarize us with these topics, and these talks started to inform me of the long and varied history of the countries that made up the former nation of Yugoslavia.

My initial first-hand experience of Croatia was the port visit that we had at the lovely city of Dubrovnik. It was there that I first experienced the friendliness and warmth of the Croatian people, the beauty of the city and countryside, and the history (sometimes violently tragic) of the country. It was difficult to believe that just a few short years prior to our arrival, Dubrovnik was the target of a fierce shelling and much of this historic city was devastated. A book that was widely sold in bookstores and souvenir shops gave the history with photographic evidence of terrible destruction of businesses, homes, and churches. But when our people arrived, most of the physical evidence of the devastation was gone. We spent several days exploring the city and countryside, going on guided tours of the city, and simply walking the city streets and walls. What a wonderful introduction to Croatia!

Sometime later, in November of 2000, our Amphibious Ready Group pulled into the port city of Rijeka. We had a very short time before our arrival there to make arrangements and plans for training at the large military training base outside the small town of Slunj in the Croatian mountains. Having completed our planning and preparations for our exercises, we started the long, five-hour bus ride to the mountains. I was overwhelmed by the beauty of the countryside, which at that time was in full color with the changing of the foliage on the hills and mountains. On our trip to the interior, more and more evidence of recent war fighting was visible. There were many new homes and businesses along the way having been completely rebuilt or repaired after their destruction in the war. Very few buildings were visible that had not undergone renovation or rebuilding. My thoughts were of a very proud and industrious people that would not let their lives and countryside be visibly scarred by the conflict. On occasion we did pass some buildings on which we could still see the marks of the bullets where the fighting was clearly fierce. Yet, the ugliness of war was far outstripped by the beauty of the little towns with lovely streams and waterfalls running through and around the buildings perched on the steep sides of the hills and mountains. Our long convoy of buses must have been an unusual sight for the local people since many stopped and observed us as we made our way up the mountains toward Slunj.

I really can't say now what I was expecting to see, but what was clear as we stepped off the bus was that we were in a most beautiful country setting. To my thinking it was far too beautiful to be a place for military training. But we were here at the "Range" as the local military called it. It was a great facility for our Marines and Sailors, and each unit had the opportunity to accomplish some excellent training

I had the good fortune of meeting Zlatko Iusic, a member of the Croatian military who served as our translator, Public Relations Officer, and general ambassador of good will. "Johnny", as he liked to be called because of his love of American Country Music and especially that of Johnny Cash, and I spent many hours in pleasant conversation about his country, the war, the local economy, the weather (it was unusually warm, and the local farmers were worrying about the fruit trees budding before the winter freeze—effectively ruining the next year's harvest), and religion. I was a Roman Catholic priest in a country that was predominantly Roman Catholic, so there was much that Johnny and I could talk about and identify with. Johnny said that he would like me to meet the Pastor of the Catholic Church in nearby Slunj, so we made plans to visit with him.

Toward the latter part of that first week in Slunj, Johnny and I went into town to meet the priest. Johnny told me that the priest spoke no English, but he did speak Italian. I have only a limited use of the Italian language, but Father and I were able to communicate with ease. I thought to myself how strangely wonderful this encounter was: here I was in a foreign country communicating with a man in a language that was native to neither of us! One of the ironies was that Johnny, who came along as an interpreter, actually didn't do too much talking for either of us, so well did we understand each other! It was also a providential stroke of good "fortune" that there was scheduled that very morning a meeting of all the local Catholic clergy in the very rectory in which I sat. So I had the opportunity of meeting so many of the Catholic priests of that mountain area and experiencing their warmth, spirituality, and dedication.

What a blessing for me! The Pastor of Slunj and I began to make some plans for some of our Marines and Sailors to attend a Sunday Mass at his church at which Father and I would concelebrate. Father, Johnny, and I would meet one more time to finalize plans for the Mass; it was very simple and straightforward: Father would be the principal celebrant, and I would concelebrate and have an opportunity to say a few words as well. Johnny would serve as interpreter of my remarks. All was well.

The Pastor certainly mobilized his people after that point, since on the planned upon Sunday, not only was there a wonderful Mass complete with music and the parishioners' participation, but also a social afterwards in which we were treated to the kindness of the townspeople who offered us refreshments of coffee and magnificent, homemade pastries—all fit for kings!!! What a wonderful experience: we worshipped Almighty God together, and together we felt each other's good will and warmth. The rain that fell on us that day did absolutely nothing to dampen our soaring spirits. There were all kinds of high ranking military and civilian officials present that morning, and all agreed that the Mass and social that followed was a major highlight of our short stay at Slunj. I believe a major step in good relations and understanding between peoples of different cultures was made through that event.

One afternoon back at the training facility Johnny and I had been talking, and he gave me a small prayer book that many of the Croatian military receive. I was paging through it, and I came upon a section devoted to Cardinal Aloysius Stepinac, recently raised to the level of "Blessed" by Pope John Paul II. After the Second World War, when the Communist government was in charge of the country then known as Yugoslavia, the prelate was imprisoned and suffered terribly because he would not accede to government wishes to declare the Catholic Church in Yugoslavia independent from the Holy See in Rome. I told Johnny that I was familiar with the Cardinal's story. As a boy I had attended Catholic secondary school in White Plains, New York that had been named in honor of the then Archbishop Stepinac. In 1948 the Cardinal Archbishop of New York paid tribute to this priest that was suffering under a Communist regime by dedicating the school to him. Johnny was delighted that I knew of his saint, and he told me that the town of Krasic was nearby. This was the birthplace of Cardinal Stepinac, his place of house arrest, and the place where he died. Johnny promised to take me to Krasic to visit the shrine, and following that wonderful Mass at Slunj, we set off.

There in the center of the lovely town was Stepinac's church. We spent some time visiting the church, and we went around the back to the small building where Stepinac spent the last years of his life. The building was locked, and there seemed to be nobody around. However, the ever-resourceful Johnny found the residence of the local Catholic priest of Krasic. Father Josip Balog soon joined us and took us inside the building. He spent a minimum of two full hours telling us of the life and trials of Cardinal Stepinac, the false accusations, the imprisonment, and the eventual death of the saint. What a wonderful experience for me, an American priest and Navy Chaplain, who had yet another tie to Croatia. Father Balog's warmth and generosity of time and spirit clearly reflected those same qualities of the Slunj clergy and the Croatian people in general.

A day or two later we were finished with our military exercises at Slunj, and we began our trip back to the port city of Rijeka. Again, we were able to marvel at the beautiful country vistas as we made the five-hour return trip. Warm memories of powerful religious and cultural events mingled with the visual beauty of the Croatian countryside made the afternoon slip by without even noticing the time we spent traveling. The events described above have affected me tremendously, and I now feel an almost "familial" tie to a country and people that previously were unknown to me. What a blessing this training exercise and visit was for me! I only hope and pray that others had a similar and enriching experience in a country that seemed to open its arms and heart to us.

SUNDAY MASS AT SLUNJ

A few days after arriving at the Croatian Military Training Area (the "Range", as the Croatians call it) outside the little mountain town of Slunj, "Johnny", the Croatian equivalent to our PAO/Camp Commandant/Interpreter/general Aide De Camp invited me to go with him into town to meet the local Roman Catholic Pastor. I had spent some time with Johnny discussing various topics, and obviously religion was one of them. Croatia is predominantly Roman Catholic, and Johnny was delighted to discover that the MEU Chaplain was a Catholic priest—one more area in which we could be at ease with each other and have a common identity and interest. Johnny took me down to the Catholic Church's (the only one in town) rectory where I met the priest. Johnny was to be the interpreter, as the pastor spoke no English. But happily, he spoke fluent Italian, and with my fracturing of Italian grammar and syntax notwithstanding, we were able to understand each other perfectly. Our brotherhood in the priesthood also put us at ease with each other instantly. We spoke of many things—it was a wonderful and relaxed visit. Father invited us to celebrate Mass with him on the coming Sunday, but since it was only a day or so away, I thought it best to delay our joining him for worship until the following week.

Early in the next week, Johnny and I again met with Father, this time to arrange our participation at Mass. Again, the meeting was cordial and relaxed, and I must say that our verbal arrangements were rather "informal". We discussed the time of the Mass and approximately the number of Marines and Sailors that would attend, and not surprisingly I was invited to concelebrate the Mass with Father. The Mass would be celebrated, of course, in the Croatian language. I, however, was to read the Gospel in English, and I was invited to make a few remarks...I presumed at the end of Mass when "remarks" are generally made.

Preparations other than that on my part were rather minimal, to be perfectly honest. However, Capt. Quo, the MEU's Public Affairs Officer, arranged for a bus to be at the Training Area on Sunday morning. I presume that she conferred with the 4 shop (supply/logistics) to make payments, reservations, etc. As I said, I had little involvement with that part of the operation. I simply announced at the daily Staff Meetings that we were invited to Mass on Sunday and a bus would be available to transport any and all that would be interested in attending Mass.

On Sunday morning the bus arrived, and my only concern or anxiety was that there wouldn't be enough Marines available to provide a full bus for the service. We had told the priest to expect 45 to 50 US Service members at Mass. Fortunately a large number boarded the bus—almost full. On the way into town, I explained to everyone that this would be a normal Catholic Mass and for those who might be familiar with Mass the only difference would be in the language celebrated. I also explained that Catholics don't have "open communion" so that only Roman Catholics should approach Holy Communion if they were so inclined. This really was the only "briefing" or "training" that was conducted, and it was quite informal. We arrived at the hall that was serving as the church, the church building itself undergoing repair and renovation, and the Marines and Sailors entered and, of course, took seats in the last couple of rows! Shortly after the bus arrived, private autos arrived carrying the MEU Commanding Officer, some Staff Officers, Officers of other MEUs that were visiting at the time, and the Commanding General of II MEF who also was in Slunj for a visit. More and more of the local gentry arrived, including the Mayor of Slunj and local Officials as well as at least one media person, and by the time the Mass began, we had a "full house". I'm sure the Americans were confused and wondered what was going on, as the Mass was celebrated completely in Croatian. The priest proclaimed the Gospel and delivered a short homily. He then turned to me, handed me the microphone and asked me to preach as well. This was not the "remarks" that I was expecting; however, fortunately I had mentally prepared for such an event. The Mass continued along and I prayed in English "sotto voce" as the local priest prayed aloud in Croatian. Johnny tried to arrange for a singing group, of which he is a member, to perform at Mass, but because of previous commitments of several of the members, this was not possible. No matter; it was just perfect...one of the local nuns played the organ, and children and young adults crowded around her and led the congregation in singing. It couldn't have been more perfect—"quaint" perhaps in some minds, but completely genuine and matter of fact. At the end of Mass the priest gave some informal remarks, and I presumed that he told the congregants that it was permissible to applaud in church because a lot of clapping took place during his remarks. One could sense that the words were those of a gracious welcome and thanks for our being there to celebrate Mass with them. Again, he handed me the mic and asked for some remarks. With the help of Johnny translating my words, I thanked, in the name of the General, Commanding Officer, and other Officers and enlisted, the people for their kindness and warmth. The people graciously applauded for my remarks as well. The Mass ended, and our photographers were asked to take group photos of the Mass attendees, and this they did. There were some wonderful shots of the Marines and Sailors with the locals, especially with the little children. This was not to end the event, however.

In contrast to our rather "informal" planning and preparations, it was clear that Father and his parishioners were very busy with preparations for the event. Tables were set up at the entrance of the hall, and at the end of Mass ladies of the parish appeared with wonderful, strong coffee, and trays and trays of marvelous, home-made pastries. With warm and "grandma" type insistence they urged us all to eat and enjoy! As one Marine put it, it didn't matter that you had just had 6 pastries, unless you had some in each hand, the ladies came up to you and insisted that you take some. "No, thank you" was simply not in their vocabulary! The warmth of the people and their genuine charity in welcoming us was totally clear. The MEU Commanding Officer, who is generally not very demonstrative, was tremendously enthusiastic at the positive outcome and told me that he thought that this event was better than all the military exercises combined. As far as cementing good relations, I certainly agree. Even though we couldn't understand each other's language, it was clear that we enjoyed each other's company from the seniors right down to the children. It was a wonderful and some would say "serendipitous" event; I would say "Providential".

CDR (Sel) Joseph A. Scordo, CHC, USNR

AFTER ACTION REPORTS

INTRODUCTION TO AFTER ACTION REPORT

After any major event or deployment, it is customary for a Staff Officer to write and submit After Action Reports to the higher MEU and MEF (Marine expeditionary Force) Officers via the Commanding Officer of the particular unit.

The report serves not only to capsulize the various aspects of the event having been just completed, but also provides Commanding Officers and his/her relief (and future Staff Officers as well) with "lessons learned" on the event. It also points out things to be aware of and provided for during subsequent activities.

Staff Officers should carefully craft the After Action Reports, and Superior Officers should attend well to them, as they can be quite helpful and informative. It can be much more than just another retelling

06 DECEMBER 2000

From: MEU Chaplain, 26th Marine Expeditionary Unit
To: Command Chaplain, II Marine Expeditionary Force
Via: Commanding Officer, 26th Marine expeditionary Unit
Subj: COMMAND RELIGIOUS MINISTRIES TEAM [RMT] AFTER ACTION REPORT LF6F 3-00

1. BACKGROUND:

The 26th Marine Expeditionary Unit (MEU) deployed on July 12, 2000 to begin the "Med 2000" cruise to become LF6F 3-2000 for the five-month deployment. The Amphibious Ready group (ARG) was composed of three ships: US SAIPAN (LHA2), USS AUSTIN (LPD 4), AND USS ASSHLAND (LSD 48). The Marine Support Elements (MSEs) making up the 26th Meu were: the Command Element (CE); Battalion Landing Team, 2d Battalion, 2d Marines (BLT 2/2); Air Combat Element, Marine Medium Helicopter Squadron 264 (ACE HMM 264); and MEU Service Support Group 26 (MSSG 26). The MEU returned to North Carolina on Dec. 19, 2000.

2. NARRATIVE SUMMARY:

a. Pre-deployment: While the MEU Chaplain was identified in January 2000, PCS orders were not written until March, (detach April, report May). The Chaplain reported in May two weeks previous to SOCEX. Having been absent for almost all of the "work-ups", the Chaplain was at a distinct disadvantage with regard to knowledge of the Command Mission and Command Personnel. However, the Religious Program Specialist, RP2 Christopher Newman (FMF), arrived in January. Despite finding virtually nothing in the way of office supplies or any Command Religious Program essential items, he quickly went to work in preparing the Chaplain' s Office to be the site of an active and productive ministry. RP2 Newman almost single-handedly worked with Key Volunteers, American Red Cross, and Navy/Marine Corps Relief preparing the different elements for deployment. He began working on dependent personnel rosters and pre-deployment documents and handbooks. By the time the Chaplain reported on station, pre-deployment briefs were already scheduled in conjunction with Family Volunteers. The Chaplain proceeded to work on a specific "Pre-deployment Checklist" with the command and family readiness issues with Key Volunteers and Family Readiness Representatives at Camp Lejeune.

b. Translant: The Chaplain made a concerted effort to get to know members of all elements of the MEU by walking around and speaking to Marines and Sailors, and visiting as many work spaces as possible. There is much to be said for "Ministry of Presence", "Deckplate Ministry", and what is also euphemistically called "Management by Walking Around"! The Chaplain also spent time in establishing a good rapport and working relationship with SAIPAN's Religious Ministry Team (RMT) firmly cementing the "Blue-Green Team" concept.

c. "Inchop": The MEU Chaplain traveled by LCU to shore in Rota, Spain to Visit USS WASP and her Religious Ministry Department to meet them and to conduct a "turnover". The 24th MEU Chaplain was on emergency leave back in CONUS, so the MEU Chaplain met with the ship's Chaplain while the two Religious Program Specialists conducted a face-to-face turnover. Before "sail date" however the MEU Chaplain was able to communicate with the returned 24th MEU Chaplain by phone. Ministry information was passed by phone and email.

d. Port calls: The first several weeks of the deployment saw the majority of the port visits that SAIPAN made on this deployment. While there was plenty of work to do (counseling, religious services), often a large number of Marines and Sailors were not present on the vessel once "Liberty Call" was sounded.

e. CCPO: Two Chaplain Candidates, ENS Jacob Munoz and ENS Shane Baxter, were aboard from 30 July to 10 August 2000. There was a particular difficulty in finding these young men at the Palma Airport. When they arrived on board, they immediately began a program of comprehensive training in many areas of the Command Religious Program. The plan was suggested by 6thFleet Chaplain's Office, and touched on critical issues of ministry. Over and above the work and training on board, the CCPOs were also involved in the COMREL projects that were held during their stay. The two also conducted the Evening Prayer as sea, and having completed a very successful time of training here, they departed for Sigonella, Sicily for further training.

f. COMRELS: SAIPAN Marines and Sailors participated in 15 different Community Relations Projects. The arrangements for each project in the different European cities were made by the ship's Chaplain and Morale Welfare and Recreation representative in conjunction with the local embassy. The MEU Chaplain ensured that all information about each project was widely disseminated among the Marines embarked and urged maximum participation. This furthered the Blue-Green, Navy-Marine Corps team formation.

g. Ministry: Whatever a Chaplain on deployment could do was done! Opportunities for ministry were everywhere and abundant. There was enough counseling to keep one occupied…some quite serious, some moderate to light in their importance. Mass was celebrated every Sunday, and at times twice because of ship operations and activities (UNREP, for example) that kept Sailors and Marines from attending a morning worship service. Daily Mass was also celebrated. The numbers attending were by no means "record setting", but the opportunities for worship and preaching were available should anyone wish to attend. There was a full course in the doctrine and Morals of the Catholic Faith offered, and 15 Sailors and Marines were faithful to all sessions. A modified and truncated Rite of Christian Initiation for Adults (RCIA) was celebrated, culminating in six Baptisms, one formal Profession of Faith seven Confirmations and eight First Holy Communions being celebrated at a Sunday Mass. Deckplate Ministry and space visitations were carried out each day. Evening payer was offered alternately each evening underway by the ships' Chaplain and the MEU Chaplain. Occasionally, prayers over the sick were requested and on one or two occasion the Catholic Sacrament o the Anointing of the Sick was administered.

h. AMCROSS Messages: The number of American Red Cross Messages for deployed Marines was monumental…more than on many deployments in the past! Each message received was duplicated, delivered to the respective command, logged and tracked, delivered to the MEU Commanding Officer, Executive Officer and Sergeant Major, and responded to in a timely manner. It demanded a great deal of attention and time of the MEU Religious Program Specialist.

i. Operations: In all, there were three major exercises conducted: ATLAS HINGE in Tunisia, DESTINED GLORY in Turkey, and SLUNJ 2000 in Croatia. Only in the last exercise did the entire MEU go ashore to participate. In the first two, several elements from each ship participated. As happens in these types of exercises, the elements were rather well spread out, and access to all of them was difficult. In the Croatian exercise, the Marines and Sailors were more co-located, yet often the distances between units grew at breakneck pace because of the successful and necessary mobility of each unit participating. An interesting and quite successful interlude in the very busy military schedule at SLUNJ 2000 was a Catholic Sunday Mass celebrated in the local Catholic church at which a large number of Marines and Sailors, Officer and Enlisted, were present. During the ceremony, the local Croatian clergyman as well as the MEU Chaplain extended greetings and thanks. Afterwards there was a reception held for the American visitors at which the local populace treated all present to homemade pastries and coffee. This event served to cement even further the good relations that had already begun to be built between the American and the Croatian military and civilian people.

j. Crossdecking for Delivering Ministry: With the advent of the "Split-ARG" operations, quite often the three ship steamed independently. That, along with transportations delays, cancellations, "No Fly Days" and safety Standowns resulted in a less than optimum visitation of ships. Personnel, Mail, and Cargo (PNC) request forms were available and expected to be filed at least 24 to 48 hours in advance of flights.

k. Awards and Promotions: The Chaplain was present at numerous award and promotion formations held underway. RP2 Newman, FMF, despite a rigorous schedule in his day-to-day duties completed his studies, successfully passed written examinations and oral boards, and was awarded the Air Warfare pin. Considering the amount of regular workload, his accomplishment is extraordinary. During the first part of the deployment, the MEU Chaplain learned that he was selected for promotion to the rank of Commander.

l. Sixth Fleet Visitation: The Sixth Fleet Rabbi visited SAIPAN, while AUSTIN and ASHLAND hosted the Sixth Fleet Roman Catholic Priest. However, there were not many Jewish personnel identified while the Priests presence was extremely useful for the two sips that the MEU Priest couldn't frequently reach. The Command Chaplain, Sixth Fleet, visited the outgoing ARG while in Rota, and will do the same for the incoming ships beginning their deployment. Courtesy calls were made with all the Commanding Officers, and meetings and social gathering with ARG Chaplains took place. The clergy in Rota, it must be added, also make ship visitations and welcomed the Chaplains, warmly offering any kind of assistance that was necessary.

m. Billeting: Both the ship's Chaplain and the MEU Chaplain were given their own stateroom. Rank was a consideration in the room assignments, yet because of limited space, assignation of rooms was not an easy task. During a special operation underway, visiting personnel of equal or higher rank were given rooms previously occupied by Navy and Marine personnel, the MEU Chaplain included.

n. Careline Updates: Each week the MEU Chaplain authored a short account of the previous week's activities, and electronically forwarded the report to Camp Lejeune's Family Readiness representative who then recorded it as a message for anyone who would ca in to find out where the MEU was and what it was doing. The Public Affairs Officer used the article each week to post on the MEU's homepage under "Current Status".

o. Reports: The MEU Chaplain provided several reports to the Command as well as to the II MEF Chaplain on a monthly basis. Included was a statistical report of ministry conducted, AMCROSS messages charted on various graphs, and reports of status and disposition of each message received. The Statistical reports were also submitted to the Command Historian for inclusion in the MEU's Command Chronology. A complete "After Action Report" was submitted to the MEU Command, the PHIBRON and PHIBGRU STAFF, the II MEF Chaplin, the Sixth Fleet Chaplain, the incoming MEU Chaplain, and the ship's chaplain for their information and use for future deployments.

p. Return and Reunion Conferences: The ship's Chaplain made arrangements with the Norfolk Family Services Centers to have representatives to meet the ship at Rota, Spain. These representatives made the "transplant" back to CONUS with the ships and offered briefs on such various topics as: Traffic Safety, Reunion and Intimacy, Singles Homeward Bound, Returning to Children, Money Management, and Car Buying. A "New Dad's Shower" was also offered. The MEU Chaplain ensured that the information and schedule of all conferences were widely publicized and urged as many Marines to attend as possible.

3. LESSONS LEARNED/ RECOMMENDATIONS:

a. Pre-deployment: Just as it is important for Marines to be prepared for deployments, so it is equally necessary for families to be prepared. Insure that as many families of Marines as possible are involved in the pre-deployment activities. The knowledge imparted will pay dividends during the deployment. Follow the timeline of the Command's pre-deployment checklist. When the time for the MEU Chaplain to PCS, ensure that his relief is on station to go through the entire cycle of "workups".

b. Translant: Having a good working relationship established with the ship's Religious Ministry Department is necessary for the successful carrying out of ministry. It is important that this relationship is developed during "workups", so that the translant period can be utilized for further joint ministry planning. The MEU Chaplain should make every effort to familiarize himself with the ship and work spaces of the Marines and Sailors during this beginning underway period.

c. "Inchop": A face-to-face turnover is not always possible at Rota. Have after action reports ready for distribution by the time the incoming ARG gets there. The Sixth Fleet's Chaplain's presence is strongly recommended because it will help him to know what the needs of the MEU are.

d. Port Calls: Going on tours in various ports is not only a good thing to do, but the experience of tours is a good "jumping-off" point for discussion with Marines and Sailors, and will enable the Chaplain to identify with their experiences. It is strongly recommended that the Chaplain take advantage of as many tours as possible as long as ministry on board ship doesn't suffer.

e. CCPO's: The program is useful for both Chaplain Candidates and MEU Chaplains alike. Teaching and mentoring prospective Chaplains sharpen the skills of the teacher/mentor and can serve to boost enthusiasm in both. It is recommended that the program continue and the supervisory Chaplain continue to provide a "plan" or a "syllabus" for the instruction period. Care should be taken to ensure timely information is sent to Commands concerning changes in arrival and/or departure times and locations.

f. COMRELS: The Community Relations Projects benefit not only the recipient, but also the Service members. Encourage and support the COMRELS at every turn.

g. Ministry: There is no limit to the ministry that can be accomplished on a "float". The Chaplain should be active, be pro-active, be seen, and be available to any and all personnel at any and all times of the day. The chaplain should not hesitate to sleep from time to time during the day so that he can deliver ministry during the night hours for those who don't normally have much contact with Chaplains because of their work schedule. The Chaplain should not be overly concerned about "numbers" attending religious services. Sometimes God is very well presented outside of the formal religious worship service.

h. AMCROSS: It seems that increased numbers of messages will continue to pour in. Good pre-deployment training will help families to not expect the Marine or Sailor to "return home" at every difficult time. Keep a close watch and record of every message, and have a special log book to keep records. Present monthly reports to the Command.

i. Operations: Troop visitation in the "field" is often quite difficult because of the mobility of the units and the distances of separation. Work carefully with the S-4 to arrange transportation to various sites where Marines and Sailors are operating.

j. Crossingdecking for Delivering Ministry: This is the area where "Murphy's Law" is most operative. The Chaplain should file the PMC requests in a timely manner, yet learn that the vicissitudes of day-to-day "air ops" can sometimes cause delay and cancellations. The MEU Chaplain should remain unperturbed through any and all frustrating events. A Chaplain's ill temper and impatience can be a veritable "turn-off" for Marines and Sailors.

k. Awards/promotions: The Chaplain should encourage the Religious Program Specialist to continually improve in his military proficiencies, and do what he can, ministry not being neglected, to earn his warfare qualifications.

l. Sixth Fleet Visitations: The Sixth Fleet Chaplains can be an invaluable resource for deployed ARGs. The MEU Chaplain should identify the needs of the Marines and Sailors on the various ARG vessels and enlist the aid of the Sixth Fleet Chaplains when and where necessary. Visits that are non–productive, or minimally so, should be avoided.

m. Billeting: A certain amount of quiet and privacy is absolutely essential for the effective ministry of the Chaplain. The Troop Chaplain's Office on some ships has little or none of this necessary and valuable commodity. The Command should make every effort to assign a private stateroom to the Chaplain, regardless of his rank, so that he can have the quiet and privacy to read, study, prepare sermons, counsel fellow-Officers, and simply recoup in order to deliver effective ministry. The Command should not, at all costs, move the Chaplain to make way for "visitors". It may be an "easy fix" to use his space, but not a wise one.

n. Careline Updates: The MEU Chaplain should be prepared to write weekly updates to be sent to the "rear" for recording on the MEU Careline. These updates are invaluable for the knowledge and good morale of families left behind.

o. Reports: Reports are not only useful to the Command to know what is going on in the field of ministry, but also to the Chaplain himself to keep him aware of his progress or needs in certain areas. The MEU Chaplain should be working with his Religious Program Specialist to see that the various reports are done regularly and completely in accordance with Command wishes.

p. Return and Reunion Conferences": These conferences have proved to be not only helpful, but almost essential for the smooth and happy return of the deployed Marines and Sailors to life in CONUS. The MEU Chaplain should work closely with the ship's Chaplain and he should encourage the Command to require attendance. It is a wise and fruitful investment of time.

4. SUMMARY:

LF6F 3-2000 was a deployment that in the MEU Chaplain's eyes simply "flew by", partly because of the operational/port visit tempo, partly because of the many opportunities for ministry to be accomplished, and partly because the Command showed itself entirely willing to support the Chaplain in his work. Without the Command's encouragement and support, the ministry would be little and unproductive. The Ship's Command Religious Ministry Department was immensely helpful in delivering ministry to Marines and Sailors. The MEU Religious Ministry Team (RMT) of Chaplain and Religious Program Specialist was entirely successful in uniting to deliver "innovative and life-transforming ministry" to the Marines and Sailors of LF6F 3-2000.

J.A. SCORDO
CDR (sel), CHC, USNR
26th MEU Chaplain

Copy to:
SIXTH FLEET, Chaplain
PHIBGRUP TWO, Chaplain
PHIBRON FOUR, Chaplain
BLT 2/2, Chaplain
USS SAIPAN, Chaplain

WORKUPS
(Training Exercises)
(Spring 2001 – August 2001)
PMINT

When one looks at the Navy/Marine Corps team deployed, one sees a strong integrated force ready to respond to any need anywhere in the world. And when the Navy/Marine Corps team springs into action, the exercise or operation seems to be flawless and done with the greatest of efficiency and ease. However, none of this can be accomplished without a great deal of practice and effort. And here's where PMINT (Amphibious Squadron/Marine Expeditionary Unit Integration) comes into play.

Sailors, as you would expect, are very familiar with shipboard life and operations. When a young Seaman reports on board, he very quickly learns the ins and outs of life "underway". Everyone in Ship's Company has his or her job, and does it well and confidently—he or she has to: lives depend on it. So, there are countless classes, drills, and exercises that a sailor goes through to make him or her an accomplished "Sailor". The Sailors must also learn how to help the Marines when they come aboard.

But shipboard life doesn't come quite so naturally for Marines. For the most part, the Marine's life is lived and battles are fought on land. To get this done effectively anywhere in the world, the Marines must be transported to foreign shores on Navy Amphibious ships to carry out their tasks. So, like the Sailor, the Marine must become familiar with day-to-day shipboard living, but not in so much detail. And the Sailors and Marines, over and beyond living together underway, must carry out some very intricate and dangerous activity in concert. Moving a great deal of tonnage of vehicles, tanks, artillery pieces, and equipment on and off a ship efficiently and safely requires a great deal of skill and "know-how". And the safety of the Marines and Sailors is paramount in all of this.

PMINT is the term for the Navy/Marine Corps training to get it all done and safely. So: practice, practice, practice! Coming aboard ship, leaving the ship, loading and unloading cargo is carefully rehearsed repeatedly so it can all be done well and securely. When expensive equipment and, most especially, lives are at stake, there is no room for error, particularly if it should happen under fire. PMINT affords both the Sailors and Marines the knowledge and the efficiency to get it all done. A well-conducted series of PMINT exercises is yet another feather in the Sailor's and Marine's cap (cover!). It furthers the Navy/Marine Corps team in becoming a certain force in an uncertain world.

26 MEU TRUEX—JUNE 2001

In order for any MEU to be SOC (Special Operations Capable) and a "Certain Force in an Uncertain World" it must be capable of carrying out military and humanitarian operations in multiple environments, whether they be in field, forest, or city. And so recently elements of the 26th Marine Expeditionary Unit conducted TRUEX (Training in Urban Environment Exercise) in Jacksonville, Florida. Various scenarios were presented to the MEU, such as hostile forces' arm caches, bomb building and its deployment by terrorist groups, and hostage situations. The MEU, using its sizable assets, planned for the neutralizing of all hostile situations and restoring peace to the affected areas of the city in which the events were staged. Surveillance was conducted, information was gathered, and troops were transported to the various sites in the city, the location of the above-mentioned threats. In each of the Situational Training Exercises (STX) air and ground forces successfully carried out each objective, all hostile forces were defeated, and peace once again reigned! The Public Affairs Office was thoroughly involved in all activities. Not only was media coverage provided by the host city, but also there was a concerted effort made by the Marines to educate the natives of Jacksonville as to what was going on with all the troops present in their beautiful city. Otherwise the locals might have had the impression that they were being invaded by unfriendly troops or that a Chuck Norris/ Steven Seagal movie was being filmed! Public Affairs also did their job well, as Jacksonville warmly welcomed the 26th MEU and showed a great interest in our activities. Our Marines and Sailors were able to give back to the city by helping in two Community Relations Projects. Our troops gave up some of their "liberty time" to help build two homes for "Habi-Jax", Jacksonville's Chapter of the Habitat for Humanity program. They also helped in the painting and rehabilitation of a shelter for battered women. And so the successful completion of this TRUEX is just another hurdle, well cleared, in our preparations for our deployment in the fall. We will be quite ready to take up the task of being America's 911 force.

IPHABD TRAINING

It's a simple fact that military service can sometimes be a dangerous occupation. From the very first day of his taking command of 26th MEU, our Commanding Officer, Colonel Andrew Frick, has stressed safety for our Marines in each and every aspect of our training, operations, and even recreation. So when the Marine Corps recently made it clear that special training for passengers and crews of helicopters would be mandatory for their own safety, it was right up the Colonel's alley! Recently, members of the MEU who would be "frequent flyers" on helicopters during the "work ups" and deployment, underwent special training. In the unlikely event that a helicopter might have to "ditch" in the water, passengers and crew have to know how to exit the aircraft quickly and safely. Special training was given in order that all who fly would be familiar with the IPHABD (Interim Passenger Helicopter Aircrew Breathing Device). This is like a miniature SCUBA tank complete with compressed air with regulator and pressure gauge.

The Marines and Sailors of the MEU were first carefully screened to discover if any medical problem exists. Once medically cleared, they all got some good classroom instruction on the make-up and use of the device, and then went to a Camp Lejeune swimming pool to make practical what they learned in the classroom. All were tested on their ability to hold their breath and travel hand over hand along a 30-foot rope under water. After that event, each Marine and Sailor was given the breathing device and learned to place the regulator in their mouth, clear the device of any water, and then to start breathing regularly and naturally.

Once that skill was attained, each MEU member took a couple of rides on a special chair that turned over and inserted the rider upside down into the water. The Marine and Sailor had to unbuckle his safety belt and exit the small cage-like container that surrounded the inverted chair. Four was the magic number of evolutions for each Marine and Sailor: once while holding the breath; once with the regulator (breathing device) already in the mouth; once putting the regulator in the mouth while under water; and the final time doing it all blindfolded! For most involved in the training it was a "piece of cake", but for any that had even the slightest difficulty with any part of the training, the instructors had special patience and offered careful remedial training sessions. This carefully supervised and successfully accomplished training will go a long way in preparing any of our Marines and Sailors for safely exiting a helicopter in any unlikely water landing that might occur. Thanks to the Marine Corps in general and to our Commanding Officer in particular, "Safety First" has become a byword in the 26th Marine Expeditionary Unit.

MEMORIAL SERVICE

The Memorial Chapel aboard Marine Corps Air Station New River was the site of a Memorial Service conducted on Friday, July 13, 2001 for Sergeants Bryon Lane and Richard C. Beaty and Lance Corporal Sean Hughes. These Marines died on July 9th in a crash of a CH-46 Sea Knight helicopter belonging to Marine Medium Helicopter Squadron 365 attached to the 26th Marine Expeditionary Unit.

Marines and Sailors filled the chapel as well as the adjacent movie theater where the service was broadcast via closed circuit TV. Chaplain Kenneth V. Lewis, CHC, USNR told those attending that all were there to remember, to grieve, and to hope: remember the fallen Marines, grieve for the great loss of these fine young men, and to hope for a new and better life ahead for them and ultimately for us. Commanding Officer Lieutenant Colonel Kevin M. DeVore offered condolences to the family and friends of the deceased members of his unit. He spoke of their outstanding qualifications and his admiration and respect for each of them. He also noted that despite the great pain they now endure, the squadron members would continue to push on with their training to be ready for the upcoming Mediterranean deployment.

Lance Corporals Jordan Respress and Justin Heath and Sergeant Joseph Polakowski spoke briefly about each of the deceased citing their personal and professional relationships with their now deceased comrades and friends. "They were heroes", Heath said. Relating how Americans generally regard outstanding sports figures as heroes, he said that today's real heroes are those such as these Marines who put their lives at risk in defense of their nation. Civilian family members and friends, Marines and Sailors of all ranks, and other interested attendees were deeply moved by the prayers, hymns, reminiscences, meditations and finally the playing of Taps by a Marine bugler.

It was a terribly sad day for all, yet at the same time it was uplifting to know that despite the grief, the Marines and Sailors of the 26th Marine Expeditionary Unit continue to be ready to provide "a certain force in an uncertain world". Americans can be assured and proud in the knowledge that our servicemen and women, genuine "heroes", are on watch each and every day to protect the rights and liberties that we hold so dear.

AMPHBIOUS READY GROUP EXERCISE (ARG EX)

In mid-July all elements of the 26th Marine Expeditionary Unit (26 MEU) embarked aboard USS BATAAN (LHD5), USS SHREVEPORT (LPD 12), and USS WHIDBEY ISLAND (LSD 41) for a most ambitious training exercise called "ARG EX". "Ambitious" because in this exercise almost every aspect of training for each element of the MEU makeup was utilized. The MEU was tasked to deal with a host of battle and other scenarios that could possibly occur in a "real world" situation. And so, for example, the MEU conducted precision raids on "enemy" command posts and weapons caches; airfield and port seizures; tactical recovery of aircraft and personnel (TRAP); mechanized raids with some heavy equipment; a mass casualty drill; a non-combatant evacuation operation (NEO); a humanitarian assistance exercise (HA); a visit, board, search and seizure of a potentially "hostile" vessel (VBSS), to name just a few. To carry out these missions by sea and air, various MEU and Navy assets such as helicopters, landing craft utility (LCU) vessels, landing craft air cushioned (LCAC) vessels, and small boats were used. As one might suspect, a great deal of planning, briefings, and rehearsing went on prior to each exercise so that each event would be carried out safely and successfully. And indeed they were, each and every one of them. Once again, the 26th MEU and Amphibious Squadron Eight (Phibron 8) team worked together "hand in glove" in the continuing training of strong and extremely qualified unit that will be ready to deploy to the Mediterranean in the fall. The teamwork and professionalism was extraordinary in these exercises, so our families and all Americans in general can be rightly proud of our young Marines and Sailors that make up the 26th MEU, "A Certain Force in an Uncertain World".

SACEX, JTFX, AND SOCEX

During the first two-and-one-half weeks of August the 26th MEU once again was away from Camp Lejeune on exercises. This time the MEU embarked on activities called Supporting Arms Coordination Exercise (SACEX), Joint Task Force Exercise (JTFX), and Special Operations Capable Exercise (SOCEX). The first of these exercises (SACEX) involved the coordination of naval gunfire, air to ground weapons, artillery, and mortars with amphibious assault operations. You might say, to use a common idiom, getting everybody "on the same sheet of music" for a large amphibious landing. It takes a lot of planning and skill in the carrying out of the plan, and the members of the 26th MEU were certainly more than up to the task. By and large it was a flawless operation, one more feather in the 26th MEU's cap! Then the MEU swung into JTFX, a multi-service exercise that had several elements and forces working together to execute missions on scenarios that might be encountered in a "real world" environment. Finally, the MEU took on SOCEX, exercises akin to final exams in school. These exercises tested and utilized just about every aspect and unit of the MEU. From planning to execution of exercises such as airfield seizures, amphibious landings, helicopter raids, non-combatant evacuation operations, humanitarian assistance events, mass casualty exercises, to mention just a few, the MEU moved along like a well-oiled machine to accomplish each and every goal. Ostensibly the goal is the coveted "Special Operations Capable" (SOC) designation, but the real target is putting together a superior fighting force, comprised of the best of our American service men and women, confident in their ability to take up the cause of peace and its defense in any part of the world. The MEU will deploy to the Mediterranean Sea area in mid-September for six months. There it will certainly live up to its description as "a certain force in an uncertain world".

Second Deployment
September 2001 – March 2002

PART TWO: Post-9/11

September 11, 2001 changed everything. The horrific events of that day were burned into the consciousness of Americans and countless other people around the globe. The country, and especially Camp Lejeune, was put on high alert. Security was at its highest level, and it was uncertain as to the departure date of 26 MEU. We were supposed to set sail in about 10 days. Now all bets were off. Members of the MEU were scattered all over the country on pre-deployment leave periods and were having trouble returning to home base because of the grounding of all air traffic. Those of us who were present at Lejeune were at the ready to drop everything and head to New York to help in the rescue/recovery efforts. As it turned out, we were not needed in New York, and gradually all our members made it back. So we departed on schedule, but we knew this "float", as our deployment was referred to by our Marines, was going to be different. The large number of port calls that were scheduled were cancelled, and we didn't know what would happen. My weekly reports on this deployment were longer than last year's since the availability of email connectivity to the States was much, much better than on other deployments. As well as their being recorded on the Care Line they were sent to the "Key Volunteers" group at home which would disseminate them to family member of the MEU personnel. I was also able to send them to my own friends and family members. So you will notice in this section: not a lot of port calls to report on, and, because of OPSEC (Operational Security), some offerings seemed almost innocuous. Nevertheless, the weekly reports were required and provided.

September 29, 2001
AND AWAY WE GO!

A week ago today (Thursday) was "E-Day" (Embarkation Day) for the members of the 26th Marine Expeditionary Unit. While a few members had boarded the ships a bit early at Norfolk, VA to prepare for the arrival of the main body of Marines and Sailors for our Mediterranean 1-02 deployment, most of our people boarded the ships in North Carolina. USS SHREVEPORT and USS WHIDBEY ISLAND were alongside the pier in Moorehead City and USS BATAAN was off the beach at Camp Lejeune. People and equipment were loaded on the ships mainly by helicopter, LCACs (Landing Craft Air Cushioned), or LCU's (Landing Craft Utility). As you might expect it was a huge event...the boarding of all the troops, the necessary equipment, as well as the supplies for a six month "float", as the deployment is commonly referred to. And it was all done in about a day's time! There was a place for everything, and everything gradually made it to its place! For the first few days of the deployment, as we headed east across the Atlantic, everyone was busy moving things, arranging things or storing things. The amazing thing about it all was that everyone had his or her job to do and went about accomplishing their tasks quickly and efficiently, and, most importantly, safely. There were no accidents, nobody bumping into each other, and everybody co-operating with each other helping each other and making way for each other. Too bad highway rush hours aren't as organized or considerate! Everyone is hard at work settling in and getting their normal day-to-day tasks done while acclimating themselves to life at sea..."sea legs" they sometimes call it. BATAAN is such a big ship that one hardly feels any movement from the sea, while there is a bit more motion aboard SHREVEPORT and WHIDBEY ISLAND since they are smaller. And so as we make our way across the Atlantic, life may not be exciting, but we sure are busy about all of our tasks. However, we haven't been so busy that we have forgotten about our loved ones at home. Our thoughts often turn towards home and we send our greetings and love to all of our family and friends. Still, we press on and we are happy and proud to be at the "tip of the spear", America's force in readiness to defend peace and freedom.

October 4, 2001
AT THE TONE, THE CORRECT TIME WILL BE...

Yet another week has passed so very quickly! This past week we celebrated America's (and the Navy's and Marine Corps') Spanish Heritage with special events and a wonderful meal. Sunday was also a great day for us. We had a relaxed routine for the day and we celebrated with a "Steel Beach" picnic, that is, a cookout either on the flight deck or the hangar bay. Our beach this time was the hangar. No sand, no volley ball, but good food, good friends, and good music. We all had a good time. Ah, time! That's a whole other subject!

Members of the 26th MEU might have forgotten about it at first, but as we traveled east across the Atlantic we moved into different time zones, and we were reminded that we had to turn our clocks ahead an hour on several different nights. The night before we pulled into Rota, Spain we really made a jump when we had to advance our clocks two hours at one time! Now we would be aligned with Spanish time in the morning as we hit port. It felt strange to many of us because at 7:00 to 7:15 in the morning it was still pitch black out there. And in the evening it stayed light until relatively late in the day, certainly a lot later than back in the States. In any case, we might have been a little tired for lack of two hours of missed sleep, but at least we weren't suffering from "jet lag"!

Rota was a "working port" for us. It was the place where members of the homeward bound 24th MEU exchanged information with us who were about to "inchop", that is, officially become part of the Mediterranean forces on exercises. BATAAN, SHREVEPORT, and WHIDBEY ISLAND all pulled up to the piers in Rota and began taking on supplies and personnel that had been waiting there to join us. There was work to be done before "Liberty Call" was sounded, and when it was accomplished, Marines and Sailors began to leave the ship for liberty about 1600 (4:00 P.M.). There was no off base liberty for us, so most of us made our way to the center of the base by buses provided to shuttle us back and forth. Various little eateries, stores, exchange and annexes were inundated by 26 MEU folks along with Sailors that are permanent crew of the ships. At the head of the piers there are several little tents and trailers set up by various base agencies where one can grab a beer or a soda and a quick bite to eat at a rather reasonable price. These were very popular with our folks. But it was "Cinderella Liberty" for all of us, and that means we had to be back aboard the ships at midnight. We needed a good night's sleep, because in the morning we had to get ready to depart Rota. By about 1300 or 1400 (1:00 or 2:00 P.M.) the next day, we were underway once again continuing our eastward journey.

We passed through the Straits of Gibraltar at night. Because of safety and security reasons, we were not allowed to go up to the flight deck; and for good reason—we wouldn't want anybody to accidentally fall off the ship. It was a very, very dark night, so it was just as well that we were all inside the ship safe and sound. Perhaps when we pass through the straights on our way home again, it will be better for us to get a glimpse of the magnificent vista: Gibraltar and Spain on one side and the Atlas Mountains and Africa on the other side, practically "a stone's throw!" And so we continue eastward in the "Med" on our way to six months of planned exercises. It's good to be here; it's good to represent our country; and it's also good to think of all of you back at home that love and support us.

October 17, 2001
MOVE OVER, KING TUT!

At the midpoint of last week the ships of our Amphibious Ready Group (ARG) arrived at the northern coast of Egypt, and on Thursday, the members of the 26th MEU began their participation in "Operation Bright Star". Bright Star is a multi-national exercise that takes place every two years or so in Egypt and goes beyond being big—it's huge! There are representatives of no fewer than 40 nations present with at least a full dozen countries directly involved with the military exercises in country, a total of over 70,000 troops. MEU personnel and equipment came ashore by air and by sea, making use of all of our assets: helicopters, LCUs (Land Craft Utility), and LCACs (Landing Craft Air Cushioned). The folks who flew in were treated to an aerial view of the northern coastline of Egypt and the lands a few miles in from the "beach". There was a fairly broad area that was designated as the landing zone for the amphibious craft, and it was straddled by two substantial settlements—oceanside communities, if you will. There were individual multi-storied dwellings, condominium style, each on its square of irrigated and cultivated patch of ground—little oases of green on vast expanses of tan desert. The houses were not only uniform in structure, but in color as well, with gray and light tan being the predominant hue. However, two edifices stood out. One was a bright turquoise and the other a pretty salmon tint. It made one wonder if these were special residences or businesses or simply a case of colored paint being on sale!! There were occasional square patches of land that were a lush green and others of neatly planted rows of trees or other type of plants. The destination of the helicopter borne troops and those of the amphibious shipping and vehicles was Mubarak Military Compound, Tactical (MMC TAC), the forward and staging point of the exercises as well as the site for the bivouac of most of the participating nations' troops. Within sight of the American compound were the compounds of the German, French, Italian, Kuwaiti, Egyptian, and Spanish troops, to name just a few. While the Marines and Sailors of the 26th MEU joined those of the west coast Marines and Sailors (First Marine Expeditionary Brigade and the Seventh Marine Regiment) at MMC TAC, there were some United States Army troops at MMC Main, the rear base camp. Setting foot on Egyptian soil brought some surprises to our troops. Rather than the anticipated sand, we found ourselves on a very rocky and powdery soil, tan in color. We seemed to be on a vast coastal plain with nothing to be seen for miles and miles except for more soil and a little bit of scrub desert vegetation. The Sphinx and the pyramids along with the expected meandering sand dunes were nearly 200 miles away from us, and there were no plans for most of us to get anywhere near them. But, ah the ingenuity of the American Marine and Sailor: some of our troops in their spare time between exercises constructed their own earthen pyramids about a foot or two in height and got their own view of the Egyptian monuments, however recently constructed!! Members of the Battalion Landing Team 2/6 (BLT 2/6) settled in an area even further "in country" close to the firing ranges where they could practice with the varied weaponry that they carried and otherwise brought with them. The Air Combat Element (ACE) had personnel situated at another site where helicopters could set down to refuel on their long and frequent flights over the desert. Thus began a very busy two weeks of joint training with many other countries, an exercise that provided a great deal of new knowledge and experiences for the members of the 26th MEU, America's Force in Readiness, on our Mediterranean deployment.

October 25, 2001
NEXT!

Yet another week on our Med 01-02 Deployment has zipped by. Time passes quickly when you're busy, and if that is the case, well, the members of the 26th MEU moved through the week at almost light speed! We were into our second week of "Operation Bright Star", a huge multi-national exercise in northern Egypt. Not only did our Marines and Sailors train at all the tasks they are taught to perform, but they did them in conjunction with many foreign troops. For example, some of our Reconnaissance Marines and Sailors conducted parachute jumps along with the German parachutists, while other "Recon" folks honed their patrolling skills. Our other troops trained with the German, French, Greek, Italian, Spanish, Egyptian, Jordanian, and Kuwaiti forces in the desert near MMC TAC (Mubarak Military Compound Tactical). Company sized units of BLT 3/6 carried out combined arms firing maneuvers, which are, more simply put, exercises that involve shooting and moving to seize a particular military objective. Our big equipment was fully involved in "Bright Star" as well, with our Artillery getting a lot of practice sending rounds down range and providing "steel on target". Our AAVs (Amphibious Assault Vehicles) were also involved in the combined arms firing maneuvers with our tanks providing support in the movements toward the objectives. All of these exercises were closely observed by nearly 40 different countries from all over the world. Our two weeks of training culminated in a display of our Amphibious Assault capabilities. Elements from BATAAN, SHREVEPORT, and WHIDBEY ISLAND, as well as some from the Spanish ship, GALICIA, took part in an effective and flawlessly run amphibious landing at the beach a few miles north of MMC TAC. Our Marines and Sailors showed the world how it's done, and how it's done right! Immediately after the amphibious assault, Marines and Sailors on BATAAN were treated to a visit by General James Jones, Commandant of the Marine Corps. Time constraints allowed the General just a brief time with us. He met with various Marines, re-enlisted others, and spoke to all Marines and Sailors reminding us of our high calling to be in defense of our nation and freedom worldwide. He brought the thanks of a grateful nation to us, and it certainly elevated spirits to hear and know that our country is solidly behind us as we make our way through our Mediterranean deployment. Soon after the Commandant's departure, we began our "backload", moving all remaining people and equipment back from shore to the various ARG (Amphibious Ready Group) ships. After that was done (no small and easy task in itself), we weighed anchor and steamed off to new places and adventures in the "Med". We continue to train and to be ready at a moment's notice should our Commander in Chief need us anywhere in the world.

November 1, 2001
LAND HO!

A week has passed since we last set eyes on Egyptian shores, "...And what did we see? We saw the sea!" as the old song cried out. One would think that getting up each morning, going out to the weather decks and seeing a gorgeous early morning sun reflecting off the clouds and then watching the whole thing in reverse as the sun sets, would satisfy even the most jaded of individuals, but human nature, being what it is, can cause boredom even with those spectacular vistas. The sky is blue, sometimes punctuated with fluffy white clouds, the blue water is capped by small (and sometimes large) white splashes, and still one could still wonder "Is that all there is?" to quote another old song. So the

Marines and Sailors set to work accomplishing their daily tasks of cleaning gear, inventorying the same, making minor repairs to any small "discrepancies", and then filling their remaining hours with "PT" (physical training), reading, letter writing (email or "snail mail" as regular posted letters are now termed), and even staying up to date on the studies related to courses they might be taking while underway. A few groups such as "Recon" and some BLT 3/6 members get a chance to hone their skills by continued exercises while on the ship. Back "outside the skin of the ship" again: Occasionally we would catch sight of some commercial freighters and tanker type ships, and every once in a while we would see a gleaming white vessel that was clearly NOT a commercial or military ship. Could it be? A cruise ship? No, not really; no Princess Cruise Lines out here. It's one of those ferries carrying people and automobiles that constantly crisscross "the Med". Most are painted white, and when you're in most any major Med port, you can get an idea of the size of these ships close up... huge! In any case, eventually both SHREVEPORT and WHIDBEY ISLAND pulled into liberty ports in Turkey and Italy, while on Halloween BATAAN approached and tied up to a pier in Souda Bay, Crete. It was good to see land once again, even if it was only one week underway. One wondered what went through the minds of those folks accompanying Christopher Columbus as they took months to cross the Atlantic in uncharted waters for the first time. Crete, while not one of Columbus' semi-tropical Caribbean islands, has its own charm which was evident as we pulled into "Souda" on the north side of the Island. We moved into a deep and natural harbor enclosed within what resembles a very large "hook" of land, a curved peninsula if you will. Passing some steep white and brown cliffs, a couple of small islands, one of which was home to an ancient fort guarding the harbor, and moving into the pier, the excitement level of the Marines and Sailors rose as they caught sight of a fairly substantial city in the distance. "Liberty Call" was eventually called away, and off we went on to new adventures. However, one could almost feel that the members of the 26th MEU were wishing that their wives, their sweethearts, their families were right there along with them to enjoy it all. Such is the bittersweet experience of visiting a port on a Med deployment.

November 8, 2001
IT'S ALL GREEK TO ME!

A week ago Wednesday the USS BATAAN pulled into Souda Bay, Crete while USS SHREVEPORT was in Turkey and USS WHIDBEY ISLAND enjoyed liberty in Sardinia. Crete, as you may know, is a large island to the Southeast of mainland Greece and her other islands and principally influenced by that country in its language, its customs, its general demeanor. The port in Souda Bay is rather Spartan (no pun intended), with just a few small buildings and a lot of concrete decking. As one looked south from the ship up the steep cliffs and hillsides one could get a glimpse of an interior mountain range with a few snow-capped peaks—lovely! A substantial city seemed to be at the end of the long, narrow, natural harbor and one assumed that it was named Souda. Not too many folks had maps of Crete so the name of the town remains a mystery. But it was apparent that it was *NOT* the city of Hania—sometimes preceded by a "C ", sometimes a "K"—about which we had been told. That city and a modest exchange facility were the destinations of the Marines and Sailors as they set out on liberty with their companions, "liberty buddies" as they were called by most. No Marine or Sailor was to go anywhere on liberty without a "buddy", a smart and careful thing to do. Hania was a fairly large city, about 40 minutes away by the chartered buses at our disposal. The trip into town was an adventure in itself. Huge tour buses traversed the fairly high mountain range over serpentine and narrow roads. While completely safe, one would gasp looking out the window down the precipices along the side of the road. Passing terraced groves of olive trees, the occasional "farm house" would come into view—certainly not like the ones we would see typically in the American Midwest—neat little white-washed buildings sometimes sitting on a low promontory. Here and there small chapels would dot the countryside looking like they were "lifted" right out of a Greek tourism book. A short walk down the hill from the bus station in town deposited our troops in the center of the "old town". The quaint, narrow streets were lined with private businesses, tourist shops, and small restaurants. There along the water was an extensive promenade forming an immense "U". The broad walkway was rimmed with all sorts of outdoor cafes, bistros, and even a "heavy metal" bar blasting the advertised music. "Decidedly Greek, with a Venetian influence" said one serviceman, and he was right. At one point, centuries ago, this little town was a settlement of Venice, and you could almost feel the presence of the gondole in the beautiful little bay. After a day of walking, shopping, or just poking around the little shops in Hania, the Marines and Sailors would return to the ship to enjoy our now famous "beer on the pier" where one could sit with some friends, enjoy a beer or soda or two, and throw down a couple of hamburgers or hot dogs all the while enjoying a variety of music. The last day or two in Souda saw a change in the weather and our apparel changed from short sleeves and shorts to sweaters and light jackets. The rain that fell in our lower elevation had turned to snow up in the mountains, and Crete gave us a sendoff spectacular in its view of several beautiful, snow covered mountain ranges. As pleasant as the whole port visit was, we still missed our families and loved ones, wishing that somehow they could be with us to take it all in and enjoy it alongside of us. But now it was "underway" once again, back to work, doing what we are trained to do, and ready to serve our nation at the "tip of the spear".

"ALL WORK AND NO PLAY..."

Very rarely is it true that there's "nothing to do" out here in the "Med" while on deployment. There are any number of tasks that must be accomplished and some of them on a daily basis. For example, there's vehicle and equipment maintenance, inventorying and ordering of all supplies in each department or section, clean up and repair of spaces and even personal articles, and, of course, the ever necessary maintenance of physical readiness for any job, exercise, or mission that might have to be accomplished. Then there's the tried and true dictum: "Practice, practice, practice!" This past week, over and above those things already mentioned, several units of our Marines and Sailors participated in a "Helo (helicopter) Raid" on Sazan Island. This is an exercise in which our military members are taken by helicopter into a specific area to accomplish a particular objective or goal. In this case, we were floating off the coast of Albania, and we carried out a helicopter insertion of some of our forces on to one of the islands off the coast, this one being Sazan. Our troops accomplished their mission and victory was declared over the pretend opposing enemy forces "dug in" on the island. As one would imagine, a great deal of planning goes into each one of these training exercises; you just don't go jumping on and off helicopters without plenty of preparation! This past Saturday marked the 226th Birthday of the Marine Corps, so we celebrated! All of the MEU's Marines and Sailors on USS BATAAN formed up in the hangar bay, and we had a formal "cake cutting ceremony" with greetings read from various dignitaries from the Secretary of the Navy, to the Commandant of the Marine Corps, and even from the former MEU Commander, Col. Kenneth Glueck. Our present MEU Commander, Col. Andrew Frick also gave us his greetings as did Vice Admiral Fry, Commander of Sixth Fleet who made a special birthday visit to us. Also at the ceremony was the traditional sharing of the birthday cake with a piece going to the Vice Admiral, then the oldest Marine present (former Marine, I believe) and the youngest Marine on board. The Admiral then moved on to visit the Marines and Sailors on USS SHREVEPORT and USS WHIDBEY ISLAND. Later that day we all shared a special birthday meal that topped off a very pleasant day.

There was another day of celebrations and pleasantries aboard BATAAN this past week. We hosted a formal visit by the President and Prime Minister of Albania, as well as the United States' Ambassador to Albania along with various other high-ranking military and civilian officials. A visual briefing was presented and then a live demonstration of our LCAC (Landing Craft Air Cushioned) and air capabilities was conducted. Our Albanian friends left BATAAN with a new appreciation of just what a MEU and an ARG (Amphibious Ready Group) can do! Veterans' Day came and went, and we remembered our veterans especially in prayer at all the religious services on board. So after some "play" it's now back to work, as we continue to push on through our deployment being at the ready to answer our nation's call to be "a Certain Force in an Uncertain World."

November 21, 2001
GOT ANY CHANGE?

Last week the members of the 26th Marine Expeditionary Unit and our Amphibious Ready Group (ARG) got to do something that most Americans only read about. We sailed South through the Suez Canal! The canal, completed in 1869, runs North and South separating Africa on the West from the continent of Asia to the East. During the night our ships, USS BATAAN, USS SHREVEPORT, and USS WHIDBEY ISLAND, dropped anchor off Port Said at the Northern and Mediterranean end of the canal. You see, even though the 105 mile long canal is on average 179 feet wide, traffic is only one way at a time. The Southbound shipping has to wait until the northbound vessels have cleared the watery passageway and vice-versa. Before dawn we weighed anchor and started on our journey towards our first destination in our transit, the Bitter Lakes. As daylight came upon us, we were allowed to go "topside" to the flight deck to look around as we traveled the route that so many before us had gone. The contrast between East and West was truly amazing. On the Western shore was the Nile delta, and as one would expect from reading geography books and seeing movies, it was amazingly green and lush. Palm trees of all sorts were clearly evident in the many villages, towns and what seemed to be small cities that popped up regularly along the shore. While there was plenty of sand visible along our journey, it sure didn't look like "desert". "Prosperous" is a word that comes to mind in describing the activities and buildings along the Western edge of the canal. In sharp contrast was the Eastern side. Right there across the narrow waterway was the rugged and arid Sinai desert with its almost continuous sand dunes, rough hills, and tall mountains in the distance. Such a difference! Naturally, then, most attention was paid to the Western side. As we moved on through the canal and the morning hours, more and more activity was evident on the banks that we could almost reach out and touch. Egypt had awakened, and people and commerce were everywhere. People of all ages waved enthusiastically as we passed by, and Marines and Sailors returned the friendly salutes. Vehicular traffic zipped by along the ribbon of highway that made its way along the edge of the canal and that was a strange sensation and sight because when we're underway, there's usually nothing out there but water! We passed small ferry slips where buses, cars, and trucks could pass from the green side to the brown, dry side. One wondered what their final destination was out there in the desert. We passed an impressive double obelisk, a World War I monument, and at one point one of the many mosques we saw was sitting right next to what appeared to some like a Christian church! As mentioned above, this was a journey of contrasts. We came to the Bitter

Lakes, a rather wide area where ships of all sorts were at anchorage awaiting their turn to transit north and we waited to go south. There we dropped anchor once again until we got the clearance to continue on through the canal to its southernmost terminal at Suez, a bustling city of about one quarter of a million inhabitants. Then it was on through the Gulf of Suez to the Red Sea and further South and really open waters. It was a wonderful day-long trip, and at one point the topic of toll fees came up in one of the many different discussions on the flight deck. One service member mused that, while he didn't know exactly how much it cost, it probably was a lot of quarters!

November 29, 2001
"DRUMSTICK ANYONE?"

While most Americans waited for Thursday, November 22nd to celebrate Thanksgiving, the members of the 26th Marine Expeditionary Unit aboard the USS BATAAN commemorated that day on Tuesday the 20th. You see, after our transit through the Suez Canal, we "hightailed it" over to the North Arabian Sea to be at the ready should our forces be immediately needed for Operation Enduring Freedom. We just didn't know if we would be aboard ship when the magic fourth Thursday of November rolled around. In any event, just like Moms and Grandmas (also Dads and Grandpas—not to be exclusive) at home, people were up early to prepare the sumptuous feast that would grace our tables later in the day. And when you think about it, there's a lot of preparation that goes into preparing and serving a complete roast turkey meal with all the trimmings to an intimate group of about 2000 people! Yet when the dinner hours began in the various chow halls on our ship, there it was, all there, soup to nuts! roast turkey, baked ham, dressing, sweet potatoes, every vegetable that you could imagine, cranberries, freshly baked rolls, pies right out of the oven, eggnog—you name it, it was there and it delighted the eyes and palates of our young Marines and Sailors. A brief Thanksgiving Service preceded the meal, a service that included the Chaplains, the Commanding Officers of Ship, MEU, and Amphibious Squadron, Executive Officer of the Ship, Reader, and Church Choir. We paused for a moment to thank The Almighty for the bounty bestowed on our nation and for the young men and women that gathered there and other places in our ARG (Amphibious Ready Group). The meal then began, the Marines and Sailors "dug in", the decorations (including a huge pastry cornucopia overflowing with fruits and candies) glistened, and holiday music played to really set the mood for the day and for the coming season. Two days later we were still "on the boat" so we celebrated another Thanksgiving, only this time, much more subdued. At the end of that day, when things began to quiet down, we got glimpses of New York's Macy's Thanksgiving Day Parade (live) and even later live football games when we were lined up with the satellite and could pick up a signal. It was pitch black out here (remember we are 9 hours ahead of the east coast) but it was fun to view the early morning sun on the parade floats and balloons and some of the afternoon shadows on the playing fields. While our Marines and Sailors might have enjoyed Thanksgiving a whole lot more with friends and loved ones at home, still our generous young men and women willingly made the sacrifice to be out here in service to their country and especially to do their part in ensuring that the tragic events of September 11th will never happen again. And so we await the call, as Marines and Sailors have for over 226 years, to be ready at a moment's notice to be at the forefront of the defense of our nation's and the world's liberty, most recently attacked, but never destroyed.

December 6, 2001
"IN THE UNLIKELY EVENT..."

Military jargon is filled with all kinds of mysterious acronyms (the origin of some of them even some veteran military folks couldn't tell you), figures of speech, phrases, and, yes, even euphemisms. One of the worst of the misleading terms is the Marine Corps word, "float", and the Navy word, "cruise", used to describe a deployment. "Float" gives a kind of impression of lazy, carefree, mindless relaxation on the water, while "cruise" communicates leisure, shows, casinos, lounges and all kinds of "tickle your funny bone" type of excitement. Neither of the two words even comes near the truth. Being on deployment is anything but carefree and mindless, nor is it a period of leisure and total relaxation and pleasure. What goes on is a lot of hard work. The Navy and Marine Corps recognizes the "arduous" nature of a deployment and consequently awards Marines and Sailors with a Sea Service Deployment ribbon after each deployment. Part of the hard work is the training that is necessary to face any eventuality that may occur while underway. And this "eventuality" could be anything from an oil or electrical fire in a given compartment on the ship, a mechanical or electrical failure somewhere on board, an accident that might befall one of the Marines or Sailors, to even the remotest possibility of someone falling or being blown over the side of the ship into the water or even an attack from unfriendly forces. And so we practice, practice, and practice some more...a "drill" as it's called. At any time day or night an announcement may come over the public address system throughout the ship: "This is a drill, this is a drill..." and the word is passed about a pretend fire or mechanical failure, or a person in need of immediate medical attention. Sailors and Marines instantly mobilize to help in ways that they have been very well-trained to correct the situation or help the injured. And everyone is deadly serious about this, because we never know when the "real thing" might happen. One of the most amazing evolutions is the "Man Overboard" drill. When that word is passed, everyone, yes, everyone, on the ship goes to his or her appointed station to be physically seen and accounted for. And this has to be done rather quickly, no small feat for a ship of over a thousand people in the case of the larger "decks." In the "Man Overboard" drill, the count is necessary to insure that nobody is really in the

69

water and if they are, who it may be. The "smallboys" (that's what they call the smaller ships) practice the same drills with the same seriousness and speed. So when you see the old movies about the Navy and you hear the phrase about people having to "man your battle stations" and moving all over the ship at breakneck speed, don't think it's a Hollywood exaggeration. It really happens out here; it happens so that we might be safe and prepared for anything that could possibly come our way as we "float" along on our "cruise"!!!

Dec 12, 2001
"AND THE ROCKET'S RED GLARE..."

The Marines and Sailors of the 26th MEU have been hard at it for a long time now. It's more than a month since most of us have seen land, and each day in some respects is very much like the previous day. It can be a little like the movie "Groundhog Day". Nevertheless, there are daily jobs to be done, work to be completed, meetings to be attended, training to be reviewed, physical training to be accomplished...in short all those things that must be attended to each day in order to keep our MEU at the ready for any taskings from "higher headquarters". Being sharp and staying sharp is a lot of hard work! So as a break and a big treat on Tuesday, December 11th we took the day off! No flight operations were scheduled, and we had the entire flight deck to roam about on for the entire day...what a boon! Usually we have only a couple of hours in the mornings up there to get some sun and fresh air. And so we broke out the grills and had ourselves another "Steel Beach Picnic". The "port" aircraft elevator ("left side" for non-Navy/Marine Corps folks) was the barbeque pit where we positioned the grills, and the tables laden with all the "fixins" were close by. Folks lined up and patiently waited their turn to get at the hot-off-the-grill hamburgers, hot dogs, sausages, and ribs, all the toppings, the baked beans, the cookies and gooey chocolate covered brownies, and soft drinks. It was a festive day and the mood was entirely celebratory. The flight deck is so huge, there was room for plenty of our Marines and Sailors to toss footballs on one end of the ship; throw baseballs on the other; and have circles of guys and gals playing "hackey sack" and "shootin' hoops" in the middle. Yet there were still other groups of Marines and Sailors standing around laughing and talking while enjoying each other's company and the wonderful weather. As one strolled about the deck, one could see people reading, sunbathing, and even a resourceful group of folks lolling around in a fairly substantial "kiddie-pool" that they had set up. Never underestimate the ingenuity of the American service member! As the afternoon moved on we came closer to the morning hours for our folks back on the east coast of the States. So we did our part in commemoration of the 3 month anniversary of 9/11, as it has come to be known. At 4:46 P.M. we all stopped what we were doing and gathered together to attend to the raising of the flag that came to us from the New York World Trade Center with the names and good wishes of all those who would send us a message of love and support and the names of some of the fallen on that tragic day. We came to "attention" and then more than one pair of eyes had tears in them and "goose bumps" were all over us as the flag was run up and then brought to half-mast and the National Anthem was played, followed by a mournful and soul stirring rendition of "taps". The flag flew there until sunset and then was taken down. It will go with us as we continue on with our mission of helping to eradicate the scourge of terrorism in our world. A great day ended with a great movie shown on a giant screen set up on our flight deck. It was really good to take that break, and now we are refreshed and ready to go when our country calls us to do the job that we've been training for so long. And while we miss our families and loved ones especially keenly at this time of year, we are continuing to be ready to be "a certain force in an uncertain world".

December 19, 2001
"BE IT EVER SO HUMBLE..."

This past week the majority of the 26th Marine Expeditionary Unit completed the third leg of our "tri-continental deployment". The first stop was Europe at Rota, Spain; then came Africa with our exercises in Egypt; and now with our members in Pakistan and Afghanistan we hit Asia! Our Marines and Sailors left the ARG (Amphibious Ready Group) shipping by air in helicopters or by sea in LCUs (Landing Craft Utility) and LCACs (Landing Craft Air Cushioned) and made a stop off or transfer in Pakistan en route to Kandahar International Airport in Afghanistan. The airport lies a few miles south of the city of Kandahar separated from it by a low range of rugged but beautiful mountains. The airport itself is a study in contradictions. The runway built to support the biggest of commercial airliners is only partly usable because of the damage resulting from the ousting of the terrorist forces, and the terminal building, reputedly built by Americans in the '70s, while spacious enough for any kind of air travel arrangements, had severe damage from nearby bomb impacts and physical mistreatment from previous terrorist military occupants bordering on vandalism. Yet our 26th MEU Marines and Sailors with the Fleet Marine Force are expected to "adapt and improvise", and they along with Marines and Sailors of the 15th MEU, and members of other branches of American Armed Forces and Coalition Partners from other countries set to work at making the airport a fully functioning one. A great deal of cleaning went on as we made the main terminal building the site of the Command Center. Refuse was discarded, rooms and corridors were cleaned out and swept, and before long we had a usable facility for work and for sleeping. While austere, to say the least, conditions improved markedly each day as more and more troops arrived and set up living and working spaces. Tents sprung up like mushrooms all over the airport grounds, while heavy equipment moved all the supplies and equipment necessary to make Kandahar International Airport a fully operational military base and air field. It wasn't long before vast improvements were made to the runways allowing large aircraft to land once again. And to the surprise of all there were still some rose gardens, mostly past bloom yet a few buds remaining, and marigold and succulent flower gardens around the main terminal building and in the central courtyard. Beauty survives despite mankind's wars! One of the highlights of this first week at Kandahar was the raising of the American flag that flew at the World Trade Center in New York, on USS THEODORE ROOSEVELT (CVN 71), USS BATAAN (LHD 5), and now here in Afghanistan. As we stood at attention and saluted, our flag was slowly raised and then it was unfurled by a gentle breeze that blew on that clear morning, the crispness and clarity of it fully reminiscent of September 11th. Soon that flag will have been full circle, returning to New York City to remain there. And so the airport will be our "Home Sweet Home" for a time, and while it can never compare with our own home and the company of our families and loved ones, still we are here as a family, fiercely loyal to our country, dedicated to the cause of freedom, and ready to celebrate the holiday season with a gusto and camaraderie that is unique to American Service Members who are far from our native land. We send our love to all at home and our sincerest greetings for a wonderful holiday season.

December 27, 2001
"IS HE HERE YET?"

Things got busier as the Christmas holiday approached our position (military speak for "location") at Kandahar International Airport in Afghanistan. More and more members of the 26th Marine Expeditionary Unit arrived and "dug in" as did other U.S. forces as well as our coalition partners from around the globe. As everyone knows, the war against terrorism is not just the United States' battle; it belongs to the whole world. Different and more areas of the airport grounds are the sites of not only workplaces, but also living areas for our troops. The Navy Seabees along with the members of MSSG (MEU Service Support Group) have done a remarkable job in improving the living and working conditions of the camp. For example there are adequate sanitation facilities that are constructed and dispersed throughout the airport area, several hand washing stations, an operational "bath house" (though most Americans wouldn't recognize it as such!), several wells utilized to supply water for washing, and a well to which the ROWPU (Reverse Osmosis Water Purification Unit) is connected and supplying fresh drinking water, all here in the middle of a desert-like area of Afghanistan. However, it wasn't all work and no play for our forces here in Kandahar. Besides visits from top-level General Officers, a USO Group arrived one evening to spend some time entertaining the troops. We welcomed Wayne Newton, Drew Carey, Neil McCoy, and two members of the Dallas Cowboys Cheerleaders. A section of the airport terminal was cordoned off and lighted and became the stage upon which the entertainers had at it, singing, telling jokes, and dancing for a most receptive and appreciative audience. Alas, all too quickly did the personalities have to leave after also spending time autographing all sorts of articles for the troops as well as engaging in spirited personal conversations. We returned to our work for the next few days with raised spirits. But soon, the emotional focus of the troops began to change, and you could tell that Christmas was in the air! Christmas trees began to spring up all over the camp. Some were lighted with electricity (battery powered for most), yet, the American Service Members' creativity is not to be underestimated. Trees were festooned with "Chem. Lights" (chemical light-producing apparatus), MRE (Meals, Ready to Eat [field rations]) components, candies, and even angels fashioned from clear plastic water bottles. Here and there you could see fireplaces (complete with hanging stockings) drawn on the sides of abandoned buildings, and one young enterprising troop strung a cord from one tent to another making it an imaginary fireplace mantel on which he hung his own socks, traditionally marked with his name. Santa was coming and we were ready! The religious aspect of the Christian feast was not lost either. With the noticeable absence of the commercialism for the season, the Christian members of the forces were better able to focus on the Gift of Christmas rather than the Christmas gifts. After nightfall on Christmas Eve a group of carolers gathered and then serenaded the compound with traditional songs in a candlelight procession stopping here and there at various sites inside and out of the terminal building. Later there was a candlelight Protestant service and a Catholic Midnight Mass for all who wished to worship at those times. The next morning the traditional Christmas Day religious services were conducted not only in the terminal building chapel area (complete with Nativity scene constructed by the Marine Reconnaissance members) but also "out on the line" where the Marines stood their posts ever vigilant for any threat to the safety and wellbeing of us at Kandahar. And so we are here during this inter-holiday period doing our part to help eliminate terrorism and bring freedom to a ravaged land and world. It's a noble cause, and a necessary one that members of the 26th MEU carry out unhesitatingly. While we miss our families and loved ones, yet we remain gladly in the service of our country and freedom.

January 3, 2002
"…AND A PARTRIDGE IN A PEAR TREE!"

Remember in the old movies how they showed pages of a calendar peeling off the pad to show the passage of time? Well, it has been like that, kind of, here at Kandahar International Airport just a few miles outside of "beautiful downtown" Kandahar, Afghanistan. The days slip by busily as we make our way towards the 12th Day of Christmas. Only we haven't seen any "Lords a-leaping" or "Maids a-milking." What we have seen each day is an increase of personnel and material—more and more of it! What was just a small operation at the airport the week before Christmas has been burgeoning with the arrival of more service members of the Army, Navy, and Air Force as well as more members of our coalition partners from other countries. You could even pass someone in the long terminal corridors and hear "G'day Mate"! And the equipment!! As the forces increase in numbers, naturally, there is a need for more logistical support. So as one walks around the terminal grounds, you observe more and more crates of food, clothing, motors, generators, vehicles of all sorts, etc. and suddenly what were just recently open areas have become tent cities. Another satellite dish or two have appeared to support the communications that will be needed for the slowly increasing number of people that arrive here. Besides being a base of operation for anti-terrorist operations, as most of the various news media sources have told the world, Kandahar has become the site of a temporary holding or detention facility for captured members of forces that may have been involved in past terrorist training or battles. The detainees come in and are screened, given health examinations and treatments, fed, and kept warm during the chilly Afghan nights. The International Committee of the Red Cross has been here daily and has been very complimentary on the way the Americans have humanely treated the detainees. Of course, that's no surprise to any of us; we know Americans are civilized and have big and generous hearts. And so the days move on, busily pushing into 2002. On January 1st we held a formation in front of the airport terminal entrance where a joint flag raising ceremony was conducted. Gliding up the flagpole alongside our beloved Stars and Stripes was the flag of a free Afghanistan, flown openly, perhaps, for the first time in years. The Governor of this area of Afghanistan along with other Afghan officials were our honored guests at the ceremony. There weren't many other New Year observances here beyond a number of Church services, so members of the 26th MEU just "kept on keeping on", ever vigilant, and always ready to protect and foster freedom not only in Afghanistan, but in any place that we may be called to serve. Such is the proud legacy and ability of the Marines and Sailors of the 26th MEU. And so, from almost half-way around the globe, we wish all of our families and friends a wonderful and prosperous New Year.

January 11, 2002
"IMPROVISE, ADAPT, AND OVERCOME"

Have you ever visited Walt Disney World in Florida? If you have, perhaps you will remember a word that comes straight out of the world of Disney: "IMAGINEERING". If memory serves, the term means joining the imagination with engineering and coming up with a new and innovative product or production. The Disney people are masters of the process, but so are our Marines and Sailors of the 26th Marine Expeditionary Unit deployed at Kandahar International Airport in Afghanistan. There are periods of "down time" amid the patrols, exercises, operations, meetings, planning sessions, working parties, and every other kind of activity you might envision happening while we are deployed "in the field". And it's during those "down times" that our Marines and Sailors really go to work using every bit their extensive imagination and ingenuity. For example: one would think that the only things to do with an MRE (Meal, Ready to Eat), or field ration, is to eat it or ignore it. Not our guys and gals, however! With some skillful bartering of package contents, and expert mixing and combining of ingredients, all kinds of imaginative meals result. One result: Mochachino! ...a combination of instant coffee, cocoa, sugar, and heaven knows what else, and you have a beverage that the MRE folks never thought about. "Hey, Starbuck's it ain't; but we happen to be Kandahar, not California!" said one troop. Then there are the washing machines; yes, that's right, washing machines! Take one plastic water bottle partially filled, add a little detergent, somehow jam a t-shirt and pair of socks through the tiny opening, cover and shake vigorously! Not bad, but one step lower than the contraption fashioned by another group of "imagineers": Get a bucket, fashion a cover with a hole in the center, push a toilet plunger through, add soap, water, and dirty clothes, and have at it, à la butter churn. Voila! Freshly laundered duds! Now comes the best part. Hanging the laundry out to dry. No Whirlpool dryers here at Kandahar International, so the old-fashioned (and still preferred by some) method of putting them on a clothes line to dry is used. Reminded some of the tenements of lower Manhattan or the Bronx, but one must do what one must do! Yet, along with the serious times of planning and carrying out of operations, and the fun and innovative times of figuring out new things to do with the ordinary stuff we have, there come incidents that are stunningly sad and cause everyone to take serious pause. The recent crash of one of the Marine KC130 airplanes with the loss of the seven Marine crewmembers shocked and saddened us all deployed here in Afghanistan, in Pakistan, and on ARG (Amphibious Ready Group) shipping. We paused, we prayed, and we remembered. Our comrades had paid the ultimate price in this war on world-wide terrorism, and it reminded us of how each and every one of us have been called to serve our nation and the world with some pretty high risks at times. But our brave young men and women continue to push on, at work or even at play, ever ready to represent the best that America has to offer to its own citizens and to those of the entire world to ensure the freedom of all peoples and to rid the globe of the scourge of terrorism. We appreciate the prayers, love, and support sent to all of us from our families and friends at home. Your remembering helps!

January 17, 2002
"IF YOU BUILD IT (FIX IT, FUEL IT), THEY WILL COME!"

As the days march on here at Kandahar International Airport in Afghanistan, and as the Marines of the 26th Marine Expeditionary Unit continue on with their taskings of keeping the airport secure as well as planning and carrying out of various patrols and exercises, one looks around and marvels at all that has been accomplished here in a few short weeks. Our industrious Marines and Sailors have reversed the old saying and really have made a silk purse out of a sow's ear. One group of these magic makers is the Maintenance Platoon of MSSG (MEU Service Support Group) 26. These 10 young Marines with their amazing equipment have been able to rival the biblical creation story and make something out of almost nothing. As the "go to" guys of Kandahar International, these talented workers have done everything from repairing every type of our machinery that broke down while in use here to salvaging from the local airport "junk yard" some equipment and derelict vehicles and getting them running and purring like kittens! And as if that wasn't enough, when they came upon a broken part that was past fixing, they just made a brand new one! What talent! Besides the "fixit guys", we have a welder "par excellence". This talented young man works out of the amazing truck that carries every tool imaginable as well as all the equipment for the arc welding and welding using the conventional welding gasses. He has been busy for the entire time we have been here welding, repairing broken machinery, cutting all types of metals for various building projects, as well as fashioning some pretty ingenious and sometimes mundane but necessary items. For example: If a metal stand is needed for the storage of various military gear, he's the guy to go to. And where would we be if we didn't have the barrel halves that form our unglamorous but oh so necessary latrines?!! Do you need some kind of pot belly stove to keep warm if your duty sometimes calls you out of doors in these cold Afghanistan nights? Find the welder guy! And the great thing about the Marines of the Maintenance Platoon is that they always hop right to a job, are always helpful, and don't hesitate for a second in figuring out a solution to a knotty problem... and all with a fantastic and friendly attitude. Another group of unsung heroes is the refueling detachment of Marines from Beaufort, SC, who are attached to HMM (Marine Medium Helicopter Squadron) 365. These hardy young Marines have the task of setting up and manning the FARPs (Forward Arming and Refueling Point) without which our helicopters and airplanes could never accomplish their missions. The fuelers have been off the ARG (Amphibious Ready Group) ships since before Thanksgiving and have been working under some of the most austere and challenging conditions imaginable. Yet, with steady and superb attitudes, these strong young men have manned the FARPs at Operating Base Rhino and at Kandahar International Airport. At these locations in Afghanistan there have been countless flights of aircraft delivering people, machinery, equipment, food, water, and other supplies. Our fuel guys keep the "birds" flying by manning the long and heavy fuel hoses and pumping "gas" to all of them after having monitored and tested all of it for purity and quality. These heroes are out there night and day accomplishing their mission at any and every time they are needed. Like any Marine unit, these men are fiercely proud of their work and their unit, so they take as their motto: "No fuel, no fight!" So then, a hugely successful operation such as manning and maintaining the airfield at Kandahar would probably not happen were it not for the contributions of the young Marines of these two groups that work quietly and steadily behind the scenes. No headlines, no media coverage for these guys, but they don't mind. They are doing their job as Marines, and are more than happy to be of service to the Corps and to our great country...all the more reason for America to be exceedingly proud of her Marine Corps.

January 25, 2002
"NUMBER PLEASE!"

While most alive today don't remember cranking up the old phone and saying: "Edith, connect me with Mrs. Johnson down at the General Store", there are some alive that do remember picking up the phone (they had "cradles" then, remember?!) and hearing a live person on the other end asking for the number of the party you wanted to speak with. It wasn't too bad—fairly quick connection time, and pretty reliable service—that is, if you didn't have a "party line!" With the advent of rotary dialing, the whole process was immensely speeded up. Then came "touch tone" dialing (some called it a "push button phone"), and before long "speed dialing" took center stage. "Older" folks were in awe. And it was the same in the military. Most remember the old war films where some poor radioman would crank away at some box-like affair trying to call another unit, or another would be carrying around and speaking into some big, clunky communication device that looked like a hand-held "saltine" box. However, it will never be anything like that in the military any more: Enter the JTF (Joint Task Force) Enabler. The 26th Marine Expeditionary Unit is most fortunate in having this communication system available to help carry out all exercises and operations that "higher headquarters" may direct. The Enabler is an amazing combination of equipment that is transported on the back of a special HMMWV (Highly Mobile Multi-Wheeled Vehicle—pronounced "humvee") configured for that special purpose. It is a self-contained unit that carries its own satellite dish, generators, electronic equipment, computer network servers, computers, telephones, cables, and wiring, to mention just a few items in this spectacular communications suite. Manned by only 16 Marines, this equipment is designed to support 40 to 50 computers (each network with its own classified, that is, "secret", or unclassified status) on its operating system and the same number of phones. However, our 26th MEU guys are not to be held down. While in Kandahar, our enabler is serving more than 210 computers, and over 45 phones! It's a history-making operation that allows classified and unclassified web access, email, and voice communication. The Enabler Marines first devise a plan for the deploying the large and small equipment, then go on to survey the area and set up switches and junction boxes and finally hook up computers and phones in the various spaces throughout the terminal building at Kandahar International Airport as well as the surrounding areas containing command posts—each of which needing phone and computer link ups. To add to their tasks, the Enabler crew must not only install phone and computer lines, but they must also "trouble shoot" if and when a problem arises, make necessary repairs, and simply maintain and operate the whole system 24 hours a day. The Marines and Sailors of the 26th MEU generally never give it a second thought when they access an email account, "surf the web", or pick up a phone in their spare time; everyone expects it all to work, and, with very few exceptions, it always does! The hard work and expertise of the Enabler Marines is very much responsible for our ability to communicate with each other in the area of operations, and with family and friends at home by way of email and phone calls—even from a place as remote as Kandahar. So while "Edith" at the other end of the crank phone is now a piece of history, so is the old, cumbersome and bulky communication equipment in the Marine Corps. We are now "high speed" in the MEU, and we are able to fulfill any mission that we are tasked with, especially in the current war on terrorism. Hats off to our Enabler crew for making it possible!

February 1, 2002
"SAY WHAT?"

As the 26 Marine Expeditionary Unit continues its work in assuring America and the world freedom from future terrorist attacks, some tried and true aphorisms come to mind. For example, there's an old saying that goes something like this: "The devil you know is better than the devil you don't know!" It basically means that if you have adversaries, it's much better for you to know about them, their strengths, weaknesses, their habits, etc., so that you can protect yourself from them or even defeat them when necessary. In military terms the saying could be simply put: "Know your enemy." That's exactly the job of the Marines of Radio Battalion or RADBN (rhymes with "bad-pin"). This special unit attached to the Command Element of the Marine Expeditionary Unit is responsible for providing the Commanding Officer with information and warnings about the "bad guys" in a very specific and local area rather than in a larger area of conflict or "theater" as it is known in the military. The superbly physically fit (they have to be) RADBN is generally made up of three teams of about five or six people engaged in various and very different activities. There is a group called "Radio Recon". These are the folks that jump out of airplanes and helicopters (with parachutes, of course!) with advance force operations specialists. Then there are some that go on "patrol" with the Marines of the Light Armored Vehicles. And finally some teams move around on the HMMWV (Highly Mobile Multi-Wheeled Vehicle or "hum-vee") or on foot. All of these groups are tasked with providing SIGINT or Signals Intelligence. They listen in on the airwaves for voice communications and even for non-voice signals which require "manual Morse code operators". Some of them are linguists skilled and practiced in many foreign languages. RADBN takes intercepted signals, analyzes them, and then is able to provide the MEU commander with some very valuable information such as the location, number, intentions, and strength of opposing forces. Because RADBN furnishes such vital information to the command, there are usually several members that make up what is called an "Operational Control and Analysis Center" that stays with the MEU Command Center and immediately passes along important "intelligence" to the Commanding Officer. Fused with other sources of intelligence in the MEU, RADBN has constantly and consistently proven itself essential to the success of the 26th Marine Expeditionary Unit's operations. Without exaggeration, our Marines and Sailors would certainly not be as safe and secure as we have been in continuing to do our part in Operation Enduring Freedom. Thank you, RADBN, for your strength, courage, and skill. We and America are proud of you!

February 7, 2002
"5--4--3--2--1--BOOM!"

Almost everyone has seen a movie or a TV show in which a bomb or one kind of explosive device or other is discovered. One of the first things that happens after that is that somebody yells: "Call in the Bomb Squad!" The unit arrives, removes or defuses the threatening device and all is well once again! Well, in military life it is not so different. We have a "bomb squad" deployed with us as our Navy and Marine Corps team does our part in Operation Enduring Freedom. We have about eight Marines who work together with 6 Sailors that form an unbeatable team that is essential to the success of our operations. It is our own "bomb squad" of EOD (Explosive Ordnance Disposal) men. Our team is led by the Navy EOD Mobile Unit 2, Detachment 18 assigned to Amphibious Squadron 8 (our ARG—Amphibious Readiness Group) and based at Little Creek, Virginia. This exceptional group of Sailors is extremely versatile in its capabilities and accomplishments. For example the members of this unit are trained to neutralize explosive ordnance, they are skilled in diving and salvage, they are experts in MCM, or mine counter-measures, they are trained to help in any mishaps on a ship's flight deck should any munitions be involved, they are accomplished in dealing with and disarming all sorts of naval sea mines, both the floating types and the "bottom laid" (stuck to the bottom), and they know how to deal with unexploded missiles and terrorist bombs. Often these extraordinary men accompany the different Navy SEAL teams as the SEALs carry out their missions. Working with our 26th Marine Expeditionary Unit Marines, the EOD guys along with our own EOD Marines have supported the MEU on several Direct Action Raids in Operation Enduring Freedom. Not only did the EOD unit provide support at Kandahar, but they were busy providing that same expertise in areas other than Kandahar International Airport. That said a lot about them, since Afghanistan is one of the most heavily land-mined nations in the entire world. The EOD unit did its job well. For example, it located, identified, transported and/or neutralized all kinds of explosives and dangerous items at Kandahar. Over 12 thousand mines, rockets, grenades, booby traps, and other kinds of explosives were eliminated and made the Kandahar airport and environs safe for our troops. The mine fields and locations of other bombs and booby traps were marked, and eventually were cleared either by destroying them in the place where they were found, or by rendering them safe and transporting them to another location where they could be disposed of safely with no dangerous effects on our Marines and Sailors. Sometimes, strange to say, ordnance items left behind by an enemy could be very helpful to our forces. At times some items of ordnance would be rendered "safe" and then given to our intelligence agencies so that we could learn more about and understand better our foe's capabilities. It also enabled us to develop effective countermeasures, so that no American or friendly forces will fall victim to explosive ordnance of any kind. Well done EOD team! Our nation salutes you for helping to keep the members of our Navy and Marine Corps team safe.

February 15, 2002
WHAT MONTH IS IT, ANYWAY?

No matter what part of the United States a person comes from, that person can tell with a fair amount of accuracy approximately what time of year it is. For some Alaska is always cold, be it February or July, and for others Florida is always warm in those same months. But out here in the North Arabian Sea, where the Marines and Sailors of the 26th Marine Expeditionary Unit continue to stand ready to do our part in Operation Enduring Freedom, it's not always so easy to "get a handle on" just what time of the year it is. The only way we get a true inkling is by looking at a calendar or seeing some weather reports on TV (when we are lined up correctly with the satellite) about some huge snowstorm in Buffalo or in the Midwest. What happens out here doesn't give us a clue. For example, at the end of January and the beginning of February as the members of the 26 MEU trickled back to ARG (Amphibious Ready Group) shipping, there were tons of holiday packages and other mail waiting for all of us. While some packages were delivered to us "in the field" in Pakistan and Afghanistan, an enormous amount was on the ship waiting for us when we returned. Then came the mounds of letters and cards, some en route easily for more than a month...almost two! We no sooner opened our holiday mail and packages (by the way, the cookies were NOT stale!), when pink envelopes arrived bearing Valentine cupids and candy offerings. Santa had hardly slipped up the chimney when Cupid was at the door slinging his arrows! To add to the confusion of some of the troops, we had just left an environment in Afghanistan when days were bright and brisk, and in the evenings water bottles and puddles froze over. Here at sea some mornings it felt like early September or late August, and by mid-day it was boiling out in the sun for those working on the decks. So how does one deal with mixed and confusing signals from Mother Nature and the United States Postal Service? "I know, let's have a Steel Beach Picnic"! And that we did. Actually it was a great welcome back for the Marines and Sailors that were ashore for that long period (for some, before Thanksgiving) and a nice break for the Marines and Sailors who remained behind "holding down the fort" and maintaining the ships that continue to be our home. It was a wonderful day, and nobody was disappointed. Flights were suspended for the day, the entire flight deck was opened—morning, noon, and night. The sun was bright and strong (a couple of cases of minor sunburn), hamburgers, hot dogs, and ribs sizzled on the large portable grills, and folks lined up and patiently waited to load them on their plates along with all the other "fixins" and traditional side dishes that are served at the normal "cook out". In addition, music played over the public address system set up for the day, footballs were tossed, "hacky sacks" were kicked around, sunbathers appeared on canvas lawn chairs, and other folks strolled around or sat and leisurely passed the time in pleasant and relaxed conversations and laughter. When the sun went down, "Cinema At Sea" made its appearance, a current movie was shown on a huge screen erected on the flight deck, and folks enjoyed the film in the mild evening air. It was like going to a drive in (remember those?) only this time without the car. Having been refreshed and relaxed for a time, the members of the 26th MEU continue to stand ready as America's 911 force to answer our country's call, be it for Operation Enduring Freedom here in the North Arabian Sea area, or anywhere else our journeys take us. Our Marines and Sailors may sometimes feel confused about the weather and time of year, but they'll never be confused about their high calling and their willingness to be of service to our country.

February 22, 2002
IT'S NOT YOUR AVERAGE SECRETARIAL POOL

When one thinks of an active and very successful military unit such as the Marine Corps' 26th Expeditionary Unit and its part in such an important endeavor as Operation Enduring Freedom, a person might begin to picture blazing weapons, low flying aircraft on shooting and bombing runs, heavily armored vehicles tearing across desert expanses, and troops charging over the dunes and low elevations with fierce expressions written all over their faces. While some of that may be true at times, our MEU would never be able to function well without some behind the scenes, yet very important, support. We are not talking just "beans and bullets" here. We are referring to a section of our Command Element that we call the S-1 shop. In civilian businesses it would be the part of the company that would be responsible for all personnel and administrative matters. The Marine who is in charge of the MEU's S-1 Shop is the Adjutant, again in civilian terms, the "Vice President in Charge of Administration and Personnel". So what's so special about this section of our

MEU and what do the approximately 16 Marines do that is so important to the MEU? One area that is of paramount importance to any Marine unit is personnel accountability, and daily the S-1 shop has to keep track of every single Marine and Sailor assigned to the MEU, and in the case of our stay in Afghanistan every single person in country both military and civilian. We are talking here about numbers in excess of 2,000 people whether they be in any of several locations ashore, aboard ship, on leave, in transit to other locations, attending training conferences and pre-arrival arrangement meetings, or in hospital for any kind of medical treatment, to mention just a few locations. One member of the section described it thus: "it's like herding cats". Another daily task is the certification on the "Unit Diary", a kind of electronic service record of each Marine in the unit. The S-1 shop members daily update pay and entitlement (special pay such as hazardous duty) entries, keep records of training, maintain emergency data on each member of the MEU, compose official correspondence and other types of outgoing mail, see to the endorsement (recommending and forwarding) of materials necessary for promotions, and track other personal information on the members. Over and above the daily taskings which as anyone can see are considerable, the S-1 Shop is also responsible for matters that happen frequently enough, though not on a daily basis. For example the Shop is responsible for producing formal Letters of Appreciation, Certificates of Commendation, Meritorious Masts (commendations of jobs well done), processing all paperwork for Medals, tracking unit awards, and writing orders to new (and often temporary) assignments for MEU members. Producing Enlisted Evaluations and Officer Fitness Reports fall under the purview of the S-1 shop as well. The shop has also processed six and three-quarter tons of mail bound for members of the MEU's Command Element alone thus far on this deployment! And in addition, the shop members also act as Liaisons with Headquarters Marine Corps with regard to many official activities including the assignment of new members to the MEU. And to put just a little "icing on the cake" the Senior Enlisted Member of the shop's personnel also acts as the unit's Career Planner (a kind of military "headhunter"), and handles re-enlistments and extensions of assignments to the MEU. In fact the professional and swift accomplishment of his duties have resulted in our Marines and Sailors benefiting from over 130 thousand dollars in re-enlistment bonuses alone! Put this all together and you get a dizzying array of responsibilities, and each and every one of them is carried out flawlessly again and again on a daily basis throughout the entire existence of the MEU. And the Marines who carry out this important part of the MEU's life do it well, efficiently, and gladly for the sake of their fellow service members. This is the kind of hard work, though at times fraught with drudgery, that typifies the strength and generosity of spirit that are the hallmark of members of today's Marine Corps. We pay tribute to the young men and women of the S-1 shop for their contributions to each and every success of the 26th Marine Expeditionary Unit. Americans should be in awe of the work and competence of these quality Marines.

IF IT'S TUESDAY, IT MUST BE PAKISTAN!

When one looks at a deployed force such as the 26th Marine Expeditionary Unit, you can't help but be impressed by the overwhelming power of the personnel and equipment, the military expertise of the members of the MEU, and the fierce dedication of everyone to continue to maintain our state of readiness to be a force to be reckoned with in the defense of freedom anywhere on the globe. However, there is an entirely different aspect to our existence that isn't thought of much by the average American if they are even aware of it in the first place. And that is the role of the members of the 26th MEU as teachers and diplomats. On Monday, Tuesday and Wednesday of this week, our MEU took part in an event that could be called a "United States and Pakistani Marine Corps Bi-lateral Training Exercise". (Sorry; no catchy, two-word phrase here!) As the name of the exercise explains, our Marines along with members of Pakistan's solitary Battalion of Marines held joint training sessions ashore in Pakistan. After our BLT (Battalion Landing Team) Marines were flown ashore by our ACE (Air Combat Element) HMM 365 (Marine Medium Helicopter Squadron 365), they got together with the Pakistani Marines to instruct them on various military topics and maneuvers. For example, our troops instructed the Pakistani Marines on Squad and Platoon Tactics, that is, 13 to 15 member unit infantry maneuvers, Platoon Helicopter Assaults, and Day and Nighttime Patrolling and Assaults. In short, it was a lesson on how small units carry out combat, security, surveillance, and other military activities. After the "classroom-type phase" of the exercise, both sets of Marines went out into the "field" to put into practice the tactics and activities that had been taught and discussed in the classroom environment. And so for about three days around 50 of our finest worked with some of the forces of Pakistan as teachers and mentors. But our participation in these exercises wasn't strictly a study in the military arts. There was a significant cultural exchange as well. The Pakistanis treated our troops to a huge native dinner and an exposition to the finer cultural customs of the country. And so while Pakistani Marines learned and profited from our military expertise, our Marines likewise profited from their contact with the Pakistani troops and culture. All the activities of this joint training did not take place solely on land, however. A large contingent of Pakistani Naval Officers as well as other Pakistani military Officers came aboard USS Bataan for a day-long training session and cultural exchange. The Pakistani Officers were given a slide presentation of all the capabilities of the ARG/MEU (Amphibious Ready Group/Marine Expeditionary Unit) and its assets, had a tour of the ship and the LCACs (Landing Craft Air Cushioned), saw a Harrier Jet demonstration, and participated in a joint luncheon hosted by the Marines and Sailors of our ARG/MEU team. Short speeches were also given, and after tokens of appreciation were exchanged, the contingent returned to its native land enriched in military knowledge and human friendship. And so while our MEU still remains a "Certain Force in an Uncertain World" at the "tip of the spear" for military might, America must know that our young Marines and Sailors are also sharing with friendly nations and forces throughout the world the absolute best of our culture, customs, and civilities. Anyone who thinks that a strong force of United States Marines and Sailors couldn't possibly be diplomats needs to come out and take a good look at the members of the 26th MEU. We can show them how it's done!

March 7, 2002
"WE MUST BE DREAMING!"

The last time members of the 26th Marine Expeditionary Unit and the ARG (Amphibious Ready Group) had a port visit was at the beginning of November of last year!! On Saturday all three ships, USS BATAAN, USS SHREVEPORT, and USS WHIDBEY ISLAND pulled into Jebel Ali, a large commercial port in the United Arab Emirates. One can find this place on a map; it's at the southern end of the Persian Gulf (Arabian Gulf) and the closest city is Dubai. Jebel Ali is a huge...no, let's say a GIGANTIC commercial port that handles mammoth amounts of cargo, as well as serving as a huge refueling point for ships and a petroleum depot for the giant "super tankers" that ply the world's oceans transporting oil and petroleum products to almost every nation on earth. From any high deck on each of the three ships you can look out and see buildings, cranes, container cargo depots, refineries, petroleum tank farms, and commercial and military shipping for miles and miles. Some say that this port is the largest in the world and one of the few man-made structures visible from space! It is a statement, not a boast, to be believed. The city of Dubai was "off limits" to our Marines and Sailors on this particular visit, but the facilities on the mammoth pier were more than enough to satisfy anyone's taste and desires. The "Sandbox", as it was called, was a huge recreational area adjacent to all the commercial interests at the piers. Taking just a few steps from the Bataan and a short bus ride from the Shreveport and Whidbey Island berthed at the other side of the pier brought all the members of this ARG to "fun and games" that 5 days were just not enough to enjoy it all...it was almost as if we awakened to a wonderland of enjoyment. There was so much to do. If you felt the "need for speed", there was a Go Kart track available; if you wanted to engage in active sports, there were basketball and volleyball courts, softball diamonds, and soccer fields at our disposal; if you were hungry there were eateries such as Burger King, KFC, Pizza Hut, Subway, Popeye's, Pizza Inn, Nacho Fast Food, Filipino Fast Food, Fudrucker's and, yes, even Baskin Robbins with all their 31 flavors!!! The local MWR (Morale Welfare and Recreation) group along with the USO sponsored all of this and also ran the Kasbah, a huge building that housed a computer terminal center, video game room, billiards, foosball, and ping pong room, a small movie theater, and an area of quiet relaxation for all. If one felt the urge to "shop till you drop" that option was available. Among the many retail establishments were souvenir and jewelry shops, clothing stores, a Harley Davidson outlet (not the bikes, just the duds), video and music shop, and rug merchants to name a few. And the camels: you could ride 'em or smoke 'em—there were always lines at the camel rides and the tobacconists. If the Marines and Sailors wanted to get "hammy" they could climb into the bulky Sumo Wrestler suits and bounce around the mat for a while. There were a few fledgling "Hulk Hogans" and "The Rocks" that were the darlings of the crowd of spectators. There were several huge open air tents under which sat chairs and tables at which our people could eat and enjoy their food, their soft drinks, and relax with their "buddies" and their "beer on the pier" while listening to music from the large stage just a stone's throw away. Besides the regular D.J. that was there each night, we enjoyed music from the bands made up of Sailors and Marines from the ships, as well as local bands. There were guest vocalists and dancers as well as our own brave souls that tried their hand (or voices) at Karaoke! Everyone seemed to "kick back" and enjoy themselves during this wonderful port call. And why not? Our brave young Sailors and Marines have been for months "at the ready" under some pretty harsh and demanding situations and locations. They have worked hard at answering our nation's call to arms to battle and defeat injustice and terrorism in our world. It was time for them to have a break for a few days. America's finest at the "tip of the spear" were also wholesome young people just having an innocent good time for a short spell. It was wonderful to see!

March 14, 2002
MORE THAN JUST "PUSHING TIN"!

Were one to take a poll of average Americans, or of most Marines for that matter, one might discover a lack of knowledge about a group of Marines with highly specialized skills that is attached to the Command Element of the 26th Marine Expeditionary Unit. And that group is our MACG or Marine Air Control Group. This detachment contributes a huge amount toward the swift, professional, and successful accomplishment of many of the MEU's missions. There are four elements that make up MACG, each contributing different but vital expertise. For example, there is the LAAD (Low Altitude Air Defense) detachment. Their mission is to detect, identify, and engage enemy aircraft. More simply put, as one troop phrased it: "to shoot down enemy airplanes." The LAAD Marines have a couple of weapons systems at their disposal such as the "stinger" missile, which is a MANPAD (Man Portable Air Defense) system, and a similar weapons system called "avenger" which is more mobile and mounted on a specially configured HMMWV (Highly Mobile Multi-Wheeled Vehicle or "hum-vee"). If a "bad guy" is in the air and a danger to our nearby troops, the LAAD Marines can eliminate the threat. Another highly specialized MACG group is the ASE (Air Support Element) detachment. These Marines serve as liaisons between ground and air teams. What they do is route friendly aircraft to FAC (Forward Air Control) personnel who in turn direct them to hostile targets that warrant elimination. They also have the task of safely routing all aircraft through the airspace that comes under their purview. Next we have the MMT (Marine Air Traffic Control Mobile Team). MMT's mission is to be the Expeditionary Air Traffic Control of a particular theater or area. Among the things they do are to accompany the Marines who seize a particular area for the landing of aircraft, and then immediately mark landing zones and light runways, and eventually direct and land aircraft at those sites established and prepared to handle the air traffic. These Marines are certified by the FAA (Federal Aviation Administration) to be air traffic controllers who are responsible for safely guiding airplanes to their final destination. In civilian slang this occupation of guiding and landing aircraft is called "pushing tin." Finally there is the fourth element of MACG called the Headquarters element. This section, comprised of an Officer in Charge and some senior staff and junior enlisted personnel, is responsible for command and control of all the elements of MACG, for all administrative matters (which can be legion at times), for logistics ("beans and bullets"), and for maintenance of the motor assets of the group. Most of the time this element's job is not "glamorous" but certainly always essential. What we have in MACG then (after you get through all the acronyms and initials) is a group of fiercely dedicated young men and women who accomplish some very daunting tasks and time and again provide services that are essential to the success of the 26th MEU. America and the Marine Corps should be rightly proud of this small but enormously important and effective group of America's and the Corps' best. Well done, MACG!

March 22, 2002
"GETTING BETTER BY THE DAY!"

In the past week, the members of the 26th Marine Expeditionary Unit got a glimpse of the light at the end of the six-month tunnel we've been in. On Sunday, March 17th, St. Patrick's Day (the luck of the Irish and everybody else for that matter!), we did our "turnover" with the 22nd MEU, our relief (replacement). We were in the Red Sea and the ships of the USS WASP ARG (Amphibious Ready Group) pulled alongside our ships. Members of the 22nd MEU flew over to our ships to conduct a face-to-face meeting with the members of our MEU who are their counterparts, exchanged information and insights into what was going on in this part of the world, and officially grabbed the torch that we had been running with for the past six months and now passed on to them. There were smiles all around, but the 26 MEU's were a bit broader, and here and there some were even dancing a surreptitious jig! We then said our "farewells", they sailed away, and we headed north toward the Gulf of Suez and the Suez Canal. The wind picked up the first two days and buffeted the ships and the seas. Then something very eerie happened. We came to a standstill since visibility was almost nil because of what appeared at first to be a dense fog, light tan in color. It wasn't long before we realized that it wasn't fog at all; the air was full of microscopic particles of tan powder that just hung there in the air. It got strangely quiet, dragonflies buzzed around the decks, and one expected to see emerging from the mist (dust) a ghost ship, complete with tattered sails and riggings with pirate skeletons hanging on. Someone broke the spell by telling us that it was all probably the remnants of a large dust storm in the not too distant desert. Then as suddenly as the "fog" appeared, it vanished and we were on our way again. We soon dropped anchor at the city of Suez, the city of a quarter of million inhabitants that marks the southernmost end of the Canal. Just before dawn on the 21st we started our day-long journey through the 105 mile long canal. We were struck once again (as we had been some four months previous to this passage) at the difference between the western and eastern sides of the canal. The western or African side appeared very prosperous, irrigated, and green while the eastern or Asian side (the Sinai, to be exact) was brown and sere. Half way through we reached the Bitter Lakes and the huge city of Ismalia, a place where ships can lay at anchorage to let ships going in the other direction pass by. But all was clear, so we continued our journey northward without stopping, or even slowing down for that matter. We passed some familiar sights (from four months ago), such as military camps, mosques, ferry slips, monuments and small settlements and towns along the western side of the canal. Soon we came to an object that most had missed seeing on our southward trip in November—a huge and very high suspension bridge that traversed the canal. Two flags were clearly displayed at the center of the span, the Egyptian flag and that of Japan, leading one to conclude that the bridge was a cooperative venture between Egypt and Japan. It was amusing to see hundreds of Marines and Sailors, looking straight up with heads thrown back, and then turning 180 degrees as we passed under the bridge. It almost look rehearsed, so well were the actions choreographed by our natural curiosity and sense of awe. A few hours later we arrived at the city of Port Said, and the northern end of the Suez Canal. We were now back in the Mediterranean! We sailed on out into the open sea, with a true sense of freedom. Again, we were greeted by strong winds and rough seas, but as one sailor said, "Better rough seas in the Med than in the Red". The ships of our ARG and the Marines and Sailors riding them have plenty to do before we start our final trek homeward bound. And, while we still remain prepared to answer our nation's call to go anywhere at any time as America's 911 force in the Med, we begin to feel the excitement of eventually being reunited with family and loved ones at the end of our deployment. We're still here, but each day is one day closer to "there"!

SHADES OF "BOGIE"!

After exiting the Suez Canal, the ships of our Amphibious Ready Group (ARG) split up and headed for different ports of call. The USS SHREVEPORT and USS WHIDBEY ISLAND went to Koper in Slovenia and Split in Croatia respectively, while USS BATAAN carrying a majority of the 26th Marine Expeditionary Unit personnel headed for the small Mediterranean island-nation of Malta, just to the south of Sicily. For many in the MEU, Valletta, the capital city of Malta, was a destination that we had visited on our last deployment a year or so ago and we were looking forward to the prospect of seeing it again. As Bataan slowly sailed through the narrow breakwater into the Grand Harbor, our visual experience was "grand" indeed. Valletta was perched high atop massive stone bastions which have protected its inhabitants from invasion for centuries. The famous Hospitaler Knights of St. John (often known as the "Knights of Malta") had settled here after having been ousted from the Holy Land and then the island of Rhodes. It is said that the King who granted Malta to the knights as a refuge and permanent home required only a small yearly token as payment of "rent": yes...a Maltese Falcon!! The stones for the beautiful public buildings, residences, businesses, and even churches were said to be hewn from the great rock upon which the city sat. The great walls that were the bulwark against enemies also served as refuge during attacks, and were the site of labyrinthine tunnels that honeycombed through the battlements and gave access to various supply and defensive positions for the townsfolk and military defenders during long periods of military siege. Once ashore the Marines and Sailors had their choice of many tours that were available to them. There were walking and motor tours of Valletta and several cities along the coast and inland as well. Rock climbing, bicycling, and scuba diving were also available to our MEU members. But the city of Valletta: what history, what beauty! One could spend months exploring the narrow streets that traversed the city in an orderly grid pattern. A small business here, a museum there, a multitude of tiny cafes and pastry shops, expanded sidewalk cafes in a few of the town's plazas, plenty of magnificent churches large and small (365 of them—one for each day of the year!) all of this was within a short walk from our ship. And, oh yes, Burger King, the ubiquitous "Mickey Dee's", and even Pizza Hut!! But ah the beauty of this magnificent city on a rock: large and small parks and gardens, bougainvillea, hibiscus, and geraniums flowering magnificently at doorways and cafes overlooking the steep trenches outside the battlements, olive tree lined overlooks that gave the visitor a magnificent view of the grand harbor and the three small neighboring cities across the waters of the harbor. On the waters of the grand harbor were not only our military ships (a US destroyer was also on a port call), but also some commercial shipping, large ocean-going ferries, cruise ships and wonderful little 2-man and 4-man Maltese rowboats which resembled the Venetian gondola and whose occupants made rowing look like child's play. Malta's population is over 90% Roman Catholic and we visited at the beginning of the most sacred of Catholic weeks of religious observance and celebration, Holy Week. There were religious celebrations in all the churches, religious processions through the streets, and many homes were decorated in commemoration of the coming celebration of Easter Sunday. And so our Marines and Sailors were treated to not only a great deal of natural beauty and centuries of wonderful history, but also an abundance of cultural activities of the Maltese people who made our members feel most welcomed and liked. If there was any complaint, it was that families and loved ones were not here with us. Many have the idea of someday returning here for a vacation, only this time with their loved ones.

April 5, 2002
"COMING UP: THE LAST STOP"

On the Friday before Easter, USS BATAAN pulled out of the magical city of Valletta, the capital city of Malta and began to make her way to a rendezvous with USS WHIDBEY ISLAND and USS SHREVEPORT, the other ships of our ARG (Amphibious Ready Group). Passover began the day before we departed, and our Jewish personnel had a chance to visit and worship with the Rabbi from the 6th Fleet Headquarters in Gaeta, Italy who had made the trip to be with us for a few days. That same Thursday was the beginning of the three major holy days that precede the Christian celebration of Easter. And so after some "fun" observances in Malta, the members of the 26th Marine Expeditionary Unit now participated in religious observances. However, the weather almost didn't co-operate. We awoke to gray skies and windy weather on Friday. That could have been a problem since our ship is so large that strong winds could really affect the maneuvering of our vessel as we got underway and passed through the narrow opening at the breakwater entrance of the Grand Harbor. But with the great skill of our ship's personnel, the port's pilot (the man who officially guides the ship in and out of port), and some pretty powerful tugboats, we made it through and out on to the Mediterranean once again without a hitch. After a day or so the winds died down just a bit, and the gray skies gave way to a bright clear blue. Yes, we were out on the open seas once again. The seas might have been open, but pretty soon we sure did close or "batten down" the hatches. The high winds resumed, and huge ocean swells began to give us a roller coaster type of ride...kind of: roller coasters go up and down; we were doing that and also some serious side-to-side movement was involved. Most had a great time negotiating decks and passageways that bounced and "rocked and rolled"; and a few sung the praises of Dramamine!! Eventually all three ships "met up" and we began our trek westward. We knew we were going in the right direction, because the sun came up over our stern and we sailed into the sunset each night. Along with the constant movement, the members of the MEU were occupied with a plethora of tasks to be completed: more inventorying of all our gear and equipment, writing and submitting reports, cleaning of our living and working spaces, filling out customs forms for souvenirs purchased in port, and readying our equipment and vehicles for the "washdown" that was coming up in Rota, Spain, our last stop before home. The level of activity and the excitement of all riding our bouncing conveyance rose each day as we pushed further and further west. We soon knew we were close. At the horizon on our starboard (right) side we could make out the faint outline of mountain ranges...it was Spain! It wouldn't be long now! We passed through the Straits of Gibraltar in the middle of the night, so not many got a view of the spectacular panorama, one not easily forgotten by "Old Salts" who had made the passage several times before. It didn't really matter, however, because when we awoke on Thursday morning: "LAND HO"!! There was Rota whose shores were washed by the Atlantic Ocean. We would be in port before noon, and our last big (and very happy) task would begin long before nightfall. We were here for "washdown" and then we would head for home. Could it be that our seven-month odyssey was coming to an end? YOU BET!!! And everybody knew it. No wonder folks were smiling so much. In a couple of short weeks we will reunite with our families and loved ones who so steadfastly supported and encouraged us throughout the deployment. And the prospect is delicious!

April 11, 2002
"YOU MISSED A SPOT!"

On Friday last (April 5th), the ships of our Amphibious Ready Group (ARG) pulled into Rota, Spain for our washdown. "What's a 'washdown'?" one might ask. For all the elements and members of the 26th Marine Expeditionary Unit (MEU) this is an extremely work intensive, time consuming event, and for the United States of America it is a critical operation. Here's what goes on: Every single vehicle, tank, track vehicle, piece of machinery, artillery piece, tent, cargo container, storage box, in short, everything that Marines and Sailors loaded on the ships seven months ago was off loaded at Rota and spread out over the area and the huge pier. And then we began an "all hands" washing of it all using some pretty powerful high pressure hoses and nozzles, scrub brushes, rags, and whatever else was necessary to bring every single thing back to a pristine cleanliness. All the vehicles were driven up on racks, tanks and tracks were spread out over vast clean up areas, tents and containers of all sorts and sizes were opened up and spread out and everything was scrubbed, scrubbed, scrubbed—top and bottom, inside and out! This was because just about everything belonging to the MEU was off loaded at one time or another into other countries, and in the case of this deployment places such as Egypt, Pakistan, and Afghanistan. Our aircraft, too, had to be scrubbed down since they also touched foreign soil or might have been cross-contaminated by proximity to other aircraft that made the trips. Then each and every truck and "humvee", each and every tank and track, each and every jet and helicopter, each and every tent and cargo container and each piece of personal war fighting gear was meticulously examined and thoroughly inspected to insure that there was no dirt or dust, no flora or fauna there to transport back the United States and possibly contaminate our homeland. In the early days of our country some of our contemporary and noxious "pests" were transported to America by means of sea-going vessels and their cargo. Especially worrisome this year was the threat of carrying anything that might bring the dreaded Hoof and Mouth Disease to America and thus devastate our cattle and pork industries. And so for four days, our Marines and Sailors worked 24 hours a day scrubbing, scraping, wiping everything that we owned. The weather didn't co-operate much this year, since it was windy, rainy, and chilly during most of the four days of cleaning. But our young men and women took on and accomplished this Herculean task without even batting an eye. After just a couple of days, our tanks and trucks, our "humvees" and other vehicles rolled back onto our ships as clean and sparkling as the day they rolled off the assembly line... cleaner than most vehicles parked in our garages and driveways back home! And our basements and attics at home ought to look as neat and clean as the storage areas on the ships! Since Rota was truly a "working port", liberty was sounded in the late afternoon for any of our MEU members who weren't on duty scrubbing away on something or other. Rota's base is really a Spanish Naval Base with the Americans as a pretty extensive tenant. There are all the facilities here that you would find regularly on a Navy or Marine Corps Base back at home. And the small town of Rota itself held interest for our Marines and Sailors. The town is one that can be gotten around in on foot. There are small cars, taxis, and motor scooters but most of our crew "hoofed it" all over town. Lots of small shops were here as well as an abundance of small eateries: Not in the mood for Spanish and like Italian? Or Chinese? Or Mexican? They are all in Rota along with Pizza Hut and Baskin Robbins. However, Mickey Dee's was located in the neighboring village. If you had a yen for a Big Mac, you had to travel a bit...how inconvenient! And in one of the little plazas around the town stood "Paddy's Irish Pub"...who would have thought??!!! All in all, it was a good stop for all of the 26th MEU. We worked a lot, played a little, and drew ever closer to our return "home". We pulled out four days after arrival and a bright sun and blue Spanish sky bade us farewell. We were "underway" again, and now we are definitely on our way back to family and loved ones. As some of our young folks say: "Awesome"!

"IN A NUTSHELL"

We of the 26th Marine Expeditionary Unit started on Groundhog Day... only it wasn't 6 weeks, it was 6 months of work, work, work ups. ARG/MEU Workshop, PMINT, ARGEX, TRUEX, JTFX, SOCEX, all the Exes came and went at a dizzying pace, and we got through it all. And we got the job done equally as well as last year...maybe even better at times. We were ready; we were SOC!

Then the unthinkable happened: 9/11. Strange. Dialing 911 used to be the refuge for folks who were in trouble. Now it was a number that had us Americans screaming for help, first from God, then from heroic firefighters, emergency personnel, and police officers, and finally from the strength of the American people at large. The horror of seeing mighty towers come crashing down, the five-sided nerve center with an ugly wound in its side, and a huge hole in the Pennsylvania countryside at first stunned us and then moved us to our most noble and generous sides. We of the 26th MEU were ready. If called upon we would hop on a boat and go to New York to help. The need of our fellow-Americans far outweighed the need to deploy exactly "on time." As it worked out, we weren't needed—at least not then.

So we deployed. But now all bets were off. The world, yes, even America wasn't safe anymore and we had to give everything a second look. Originally it was going to be a great winter "float", with lots to see and do, lots of good ports to visit (imagine Rome at Christmas?!!). Yes, all bets were off. We did do some exercises: Bright Star in Egypt for example, but not much more...we just waited. And port calls? Try just one—turned out O.K. though.

Then the word came: Through the "ditch" (Suez Canal) and into the North Arabian Sea. Word came again and there we were: "Liberating" and occupying several places in Afghanistan...the terrorists weren't going to have an easy time of it...we were going to make sure of that...too many memories of burning buildings and faces in agony. Christmas in Kandahar: no, it wasn't Rome, but it was O.K. We were with our buddies and we were with our God; and HE would have to take care of our families. And the American people—so generous, so supportive of all we were doing, so much a help to get us through what we had to get through. And some of our comrades died...we grieved as all America had a few months before on 9/11.

Then it was over. The Army and Air Force came and the 26th MEU moved back to the ships ready to go again wherever and whenever our nation called. No more calls came...back to the "Med", a port call and then the long trek home.

So we did it. And now we're home again. Some call us "heroes", but we only did our job. America called on us to do what we are trained to do. How could we even hesitate? We are Marines and Sailors of the 26th Marine Expeditionary Unit and we would never let our county and our fellow Americans down. That's what we are all about; that's what America is all about. Courage under fire; hearts as big as a house. God Bless the 26th MEU and God Bless America!

J.A. SCORDO
26TH MEU Chaplain

After Action Reports

INTRODUCTION

The following are two After Action Reports: One covering the totality of the deployment lasting seven months, and the other that deals with OPERATION ENDURING FREEDOM. While similar, they should give a good sense of what went on during the entirety of the deployment as well as the more detailed discussion of our time in Afghanistan.

16 MAR 02

From: MEU Chaplain, 26th Marine Expeditionary Unit
To: Command Chaplain, II Marine Expeditionary Force
Via: Commanding Officer, 26th Marine Expeditionary Unit
Subj: 26TH MEU COMMAND ELEMENT COMMAND RELIGIOUS MINISTRIES TEAM [RMT] AFTER-ACTION FOR OPERATION ENDURING FREEDOM 2002.

1. BACKGROUND:

The 26th Marine Expeditionary Unit (MEU) deployed to Pakistan and also to Forward Operating Base Rhino, Kandahar International Airport, Kabul, and Khowst in Afghanistan in support of Operation Enduring freedom.

2. NARRATIVE SUMMARY:

Transportation and Billeting: The MEU Command Element Chaplain and Religious Program Specialist (RP) Religious Ministry Team (RMT) left USS BATAAN on 13 December 2001 via LCAC to the beach in Pakistan and was transported by 5 ton vehicle to an airfield. That evening the RMT moved by KC 130 aircraft to a Forward Arming and Refueling Point (FARP) in Pakistan. They remained there until transportation was available to Kandahar. The RMT arrived 16 December at Khandahar International Airport in Afghanistan, and upon arrival was billeted in the airport terminal.

Working Spaces: Because of limited working spaces, the Chaplain and RP shared an office with the 26 MEU Staff Judge Advocate. The MEU Public Affairs Officer was also slated to use this same place, but found another area out of which to operate. The Chaplain/SJA space was also used for daily Catholic Masses as well as billeting.

Ministry: The Chaplain celebrated Roman Catholic Mass daily and several times each weekend, administered the Sacrament of Reconciliation (Confession), prayed privately with Marines and Sailors, visited and prayed over the sick in the medical spaces, and spent the remainder of his time visiting various living and working spaces of the MEU, and talking with Marines and Sailors at various locations in and around the airport terminal and different camp sites on the battle lines. Two Memorial Services were conducted during the stay at Kandahar remembering a total of nine Marines who lost their lives in two separate aircraft accidents. Informal sessions for Critical Incident Stress Debriefing (CISD) for members of the rescue/recovery teams sent to the sites of the aircraft crashes. The RMT had religious articles, supplies, reading materials, and other aids to ministry available for distribution to the members of the MEU. The articles and reading materials were distributed rather quickly and the supply ran out much sooner than either the Chaplain or RP expected. Candles that were useful and sometimes necessary for services were obtained through the Logistic Section.

Collateral Ministry: The MEU Chaplain organized and led Ecumenical / Joint Christmas Caroling event at Khandahar. A huge amount of "holiday" cards and letters as well as many "Care Packages" of candies, personal hygiene articles, and miscellaneous items were delivered to the Chaplain's Office to be distributed. This distribution was done with great dispatch.

AMCROSS Messages: There were 54 messages from the American Red Cross received during this time away from USS Bataan. The messages came by way of 26 MEU Communication Center. After each message was received, the information was recorded in a log book designated especially for that purpose, appropriate action was taken on the message, and a response was sent to The American Red Cross via message traffic.

Courtesy Calls: The Chaplain and RP made it a point to become acquainted with other Joint Forces' and Coalition Forces' Religious Program Staff as well as being available to support them in ministry when the need arose.

Media: There was impressive representation of every type of media from a wide selection of America's press and video as well as those from other nations. They documented many of the religious activities and services held at the airport in Kandahar.

Official Visitors: At Christmas the Chaplain of the Marine Corps, the NAVCENT, and the SURFPAC chaplains visited Forward Operating Base Rhino, and Kandahar International Airport. Care was taken to afford them an opportunity to conduct religious services and visitations during their brief stay.

Religious Accommodation: A mosque and two other "sacred" (or at least considered as such) places were located on the grounds of Kandahar International Airport. Two Muslim Corpsman approached the chaplain with a serious and legitimate concern. In one of the holy places there appeared to be the beginnings of occupation of those spaces for office/billeting areas. This is clearly a violation of Muslim religious sensitivities if not religious practice and law. The Command Element Chaplain brought the entire matter to the attention of the MEU Commander who in turn declared all such religious sites as "off limits" to anyone or anything that was not connected with Muslim religious worship or meetings. The Battalion Landing Team Chaplain co-operated with the Corpsmen concerned, and together they accomplished the cleaning and readying of the spaces for worship. American and Afghan Muslims utilized the space thereafter for prayer and worship.

3. LESSONS LEARNED/ RECOMMENDATIONS:

Transportation and Billeting: Often in a restricted area such as Kandahar International Airport transportation is primarily by foot. This can quite helpful in some instances as it provides "high visibility" of the RMT and "advertises" the availability of Chaplain to all who should desire any form of ministry. Whenever possible the Chaplain and Religious Program Specialist should have their own billeting spaces to afford an opportunity to deliver better and more efficient ministry, especially in the area of privacy and confidentiality.

Working Spaces: While the lack of office space did not impede the delivery of effective ministry during this period, the Chaplain and Religious Program Specialist should have their own office space to accommodate each client with privacy while counseling. The MEU Staff Judge Advocate was very accommodating in vacating the shared office space each day for the celebration of Roman Catholic Mass. Had the MEU Public Affairs Officer also shared that space as was the intention in the designation and allocation of office spaces, there certainly would never have been enough room to accommodate the three departments and each one's extensive work.

Ministry: The Chaplain and RP's visibility and availability clearly helped in the delivery of ministry. The Marines and Sailors knew the RMT was there and felt comfortable in approaching the team. Constant vigilance is necessary to ensure that all religious worship needs are met, especially those of the troops that must stand watch "on the line." Be aware that deaths can happen at any time, and the RMT must be prepared to organize and conduct a Memorial Service at very short notice. Be prepared to conduct CISD (Critical Incident Stress Debriefing) debriefing sessions when needed. Ensure ecclesiastical supplies (i.e. Bibles, Diverse Pamphlets, Communion Wine and Wafers, Memorial Services Bulletins, Ecclesiastical linens and Miscellaneous Supplies) are packed to provide for ministry in excess of 30 days. This will allow the RMT to better serve troops with their Religion preferences and other spiritual support. Be alert to opportunities available to obtain supplies locally as in the case of candles.

Collateral Ministry: Be open to and take advantage of any suggestion that would enhance the delivery of ministry in situations such as that at Kandahar. The suggestion for Christmas Caroling came from one of the Marines, and the RMT "jumped" on the idea to organize the event and lead it when the time came.

It resulted in a great success. Be prepared to distribute mail and "care packages" immediately as they are received. Know (keep written records if necessary) who had already received packages and mail and ensure an equitable distribution of these treats.

AMCROSS Messages: The Chaplain and RP should expect Red Cross Messages in abundance in activities such as Operation Enduring Freedom. Care must be taken to log all messages, to notify all parties concerned, and to draft an appropriate response to each message.

Courtesy Calls: One cannot emphasize too much the need for co-operation among joint forces' RMT especially in this age of joint forces/ministry. Besides providing new opportunities for ministry, it cannot help but to enhance the reputation of the MEU when the RMT makes courtesy calls with Joint Forces' and Coalition Forces' Chaplains and Staff. A standoffish or unfriendly demeanor reflects badly not only on the Chaplain's Department, but also on the Marine Corps Command as well.

Media: The RMT should not be surprised to see a good representation of various media present at sites such as those in Pakistan, and Afghanistan especially when important events such as Operation Enduring Freedom takes place. The RMT team should take full advantage of the media's presence, and encourage media coverage of religious and other ministry related events while maintaining a respectful religious atmosphere at those services. It is good for the American public to know that the young men and women of the military forces have the opportunity to take advantage of their right to free exercise of religion. The media by giving the RMT frequent and broad coverage did a magnificent job in also telling the Chaplain/RP Team ministry story, often better than the Chaplain Corps itself did.

Official Visitors: The RMT can expect Official Visitors in high visibility places such as Kandahar. Be prepared to welcome all of them, and if necessary arrange for billeting and feeding. Escort these VIP visitors on all courtesy calls to various commanders.

Religious Accommodation: Be aware that uninformed and well-meaning troops may inadvertently violate religious "worship space." Be prepared to act immediately if and when these situations become known. Understand that such religious accommodation and awareness to sensitivities can pay big dividends when it comes to public relations and good will from foreign nationals of the Muslim faith.

4. SUMMARY:

Operation Enduring Freedom proved to be a challenging but highly successful experience for the RMT. Ministry was available for and provided to all MEU, Joint Forces and Coalition Forces personnel at the various sites involved in the operations.

The message that "God was alive and well" was clear by the presence and activity of the RMT and that message was amplified and delivered to the people of the United States and other countries of the world through the work of the civilian media. The Chaplain/RP Religious Ministry Team was even more visible than ever and their continued availability to not only the Marines and Sailors of the 26th Marine Expeditionary Unit but also to members of all forces present was clear to all and taken advantage of by many.

J. A. SCORDO
CDR, CHC, USNR

12 April 02

From: MEU Chaplain, 26th Marine Expeditionary Unit
To: Command Chaplain, II Marine Expeditionary Force
Via: Commanding Officer, 26th Marine Expeditionary Unit
Subj: 26TH MEU COMMAND ELEMENT COMMAND RELIGIOUS MINISTRIES TEAM (RMT) AFTER-ACTION REPORT FOR LF6F 1-02
Encl: (1) Ministry Statistics
          AMCROSS Charts and Graphs
          After Action Report for OPERATION ENDURING FREEDOM.

1. BACKGROUND:

The 26th Marine Expeditionary Unit Special Operations Capable (MEU SOC) deployed on September 20, 2001 for a six-month deployment in the Mediterranean which eventually was extended to a seven-month deployment. The Amphibious Ready Group (ARG) was composed of three ships: USS BATAAN (LHD 5), USS SHREVEPORT (LPD 12), and USS WHIDBEY ISLAND (LSD 41). The 26th MEU was composed of four units. The Command Element (CE) and three Major Subordinate Elements (MSEs): Battalion Landing Team 3/6(BLT 3/6); Air Combat Element , Marine Medium Helicopter Squadron 365 (ACE, HMM 365), and MEU Service Support Group 26 (MSSG 26). The MEU was originally scheduled to return to the United States on March 18, 2002, but, in the end, returned on April 18, 2002.

2. NARRATIVE SUMMARY:

Pre-deployment: Shortly after a new Commanding Officer, Colonel Andrew Frick, took command of 26 MEU, the unit began the full cycle of "workups". Religious Program Specialist First Class (RP1) Eddie B. Williams (SW/FMF) arrived and completed the formation of the 26th MEU Religious Ministry Team (RMT). Along with Commander (Select) Chaplain Joseph A. Scordo, the two took part in all pre-deployment activities and exercises underway and away from garrison as well as helped in the meetings and activities of the KEY VOLUNTEER network at home. Emergency Data Forms were created, distributed and collected; Navy/Marine Corps Relief Authorization Forms were distributed and collected; regularly updated Rosters were compiled; the pre-deployment book was worked on; and all supplies for the deployment were ordered. While underway during this time the MEU RMT forged a close and effective working relationship with not only the MEU MSE Chaplains, but also with the Chaplains on the various ships. The MEU Chaplain was promoted to the rank of Commander (O5) on June 1, 2001. Shortly before the MEU was to deploy, the RMT participated in the MEU CE's family pre-deployment brief. On September 11, 2001 the 26th MEU was put on alert to be ready to go to New York City to help out after the terrorist attacks there. However, the MEU's help was, in fact, not needed at that point, so the MEU deployed to the Mediterranean on schedule.

Translant: While making the Atlantic crossing, the Chaplain and RP continued their getting to know more and more of the Marines and Sailors of the various elements of the MEU as well as those attached to the ships. There is much to be said for "Deckplate Ministry", or "Ministry of Presence", or what is sometimes called (with tongue in cheek): "Management by Walking Around"! The accessibility and familiarity with the Chaplain and his RP can make it easier for the Marine and Sailor to ask for help if the need arises during the deployment. The MEU RMT also continued to forge a strong working relationship with the ships' RMTs as well.

Turnovers: The turnovers with the outgoing and incoming MEU Chaplains at the beginning and end of the deployment were done by Video Teleconferences. While there was not much "new" from the Chaplain who left the "Med" when we "inchopped", there was a good deal of information to be passed to the Chaplain of the MEU that relieved 26 MEU at the "turnover" time.

Portcalls: Because of the operational tempo, the heightened security states at all military bases, overseas or at home, and because of the increased threat at many ports previously considered "safe" in the Mediterranean, not many port visits were scheduled. There was only one port visit after EXERCISE BRIGHT STAR in Egypt and before being called to transit the Suez Canal to be prepared to take part in OPERATION ENDURING FREEDOM.

CCPO: In the past, Chaplain Candidate Program Officers (CCPO) would ride the ships to get "on the job training" while in seminary formation. During this deployment, because of operational tempo and security considerations, there were no CCPO visits and training.

COMRELS: Again, because of operational tempo and security considerations there were no Community Relations projects undertaken by the Marines and Sailors of USS BATAAN, while some opportunities presented themselves to the other ships of the ARG.

Ministry: Whatever a Chaplain could do on deployment was done! Opportunities for ministry were everywhere and abundant. There was enough counseling to keep the Chaplain occupied and the sessions involved matters quite serious at times and less serious at others. Along with the Roman Catholic Chaplain for BATAAN, the MEU Chaplain celebrated daily Mass and twice on weekends. The numbers in attendance steadily increased as the deployment progressed. There was a full course in the Doctrine and Morals of the Catholic Faith offered and many Marines and Sailors attended. A modified Rite of Christian Initiation for Adults (RCIA) was celebrated culminating in 26 Baptisms, Professions of Faith, Confirmations, and First Holy Communions. Deckplate ministry and space visitations were carried out each day. Evening Prayer at Sea was offered on a regular basis, taking turns with the ship's chaplains. On a regular basis requests for prayers over the sick were made, and the Chaplain visited the medical spaces to visit and pray over the sick. The other MEU Chaplains as well as the ships' Chaplains provided religious services in the Protestant traditions, conducted various training sessions, religious classes, and Bible Studies, and at the end of the deployment the Protestant Chaplains and some RPs conducted a Revival Worship Series while in port at Rota, Spain. When chaplains were not available to provide some particular religious ministry to the ships in the ARG, there were faith specific Lay Leaders who had been trained and appointed to fill that need.

AMCROSS MESSAGES: There were large numbers of American Red Cross messages for deployed Marines and Sailors of the 26th MEU. Each message received was duplicated, delivered to the respective commands, logged and tracked, delivered to the MEU Commanding Officer and Executive Officer and Sergeant Major, and responded to in a timely manner. It demanded a great deal of attention and time of the MEU Religious Program Specialist who never "dropped the ball" on any of the numerous messages received during the deployment.

Operations: There were two major events that the MEU Religious Ministry Team participated in: Exercise BRIGHT STAR in Egypt and OPERATION ENDURING FREEDOM. An After Action Report for the latter is enclosed with this report.

Crossdecking for Delivering Ministry: With "Split ARG" operations, "no fly days", and other obstacles arising, the MEU Catholic Chaplain did not make frequent trips to ARG shipping at the beginning of the deployment. The BLT

Commander, desiring his Catholic personnel to have "Catholic coverage" on the other ships of the ARG, appointed the BLT Air Officer to work directly with the MEU Chaplain to arrange regular flights to the other ships. This arrangement worked out very well, and the BLT Air Officer made every effort to aid and accommodate the MEU Chaplain in his attempts to reach the other ships.

Awards and Promotions: The Chaplain was present at numerous award and promotion formations held while underway. RP1 Williams (SW/FMF), despite a rigorous schedule in his day-to-day duties, completed his studies, successfully passed written examinations and oral boards and was awarded the Air Warfare pin. Considering the amount of regular workload, as well as standing watch in the library daily and "rigging for religious services", his accomplishment was extraordinary.

Collateral Duties: One of the duties entrusted to the RMT this deployment was the distribution and tracking of the huge amount of mail and "care packages" or "smiles" that were sent to the MEU for the Marines and Sailors. Because of OPERATION ENDURING FREEDOM, the American public's awareness of the MEU's part in it, and because we were deployed during the Christmas holiday season, more packages and letters arrived than had ever been seen in previous deployments. The Chaplain also wrote many "Thank You" notes and letters to the generous donors thereby enhancing the reputation of the MEU throughout the United States.

Billeting: The Chaplain was given a stateroom where he not only slept at night, but also conducted most of his non-worship "business", i.e. counseling, spiritual direction, administrative duties. The Troop Chaplain's Office, while situated in a convenient location near the ship's Mess Decks, was far too noisy for regular conversation tone—one would almost have to shout to be heard—and the slamming of nearby doors produced reverberations that were sometimes close to painful. The location of the stateroom close to the ship's gym made for easy access for officer and enlisted alike. During OPERATION ENDURING FREEDOM, when the Chaplain was ashore, his stateroom was used by a female civilian visitor and later two Marine Corps Majors.

Careline Updates: Each week from the beginning of the deployment, the MEU Chaplain authored a short account of the previous week's activities, and electronically forwarded the report to Camp Lejeune's Family Readiness representative who then recorded it on the MEU's "Careline" as a message for anyone who would call in to find out where the MEU was and what it was doing. The KEY VOLUNTEERS co-ordinators were also recipients of the weekly update. The Public Affairs Officer also used the article each week to post on the MEU's homepage under "Current Status". This enabled family and friends of the deployed Marines and Sailors, as well as the American public at large, to have a good idea of what was happening during our deployment. The Chaplain, dubbing his weekly reports "Happy Grams", also used them as weekly electronic mailings to family, friends, and colleagues back in the United States. Many of these recipients, in turn, forwarded these messages to other friends, and the exploits and accomplishments of the 26th MEU got widespread recognition. A civilian newspaper in Ohio received the MEU Chaplain's permission to publish them weekly as "Postcards to the States".

Return and Reunion Conferences: The Ship's Chaplain made arrangements with the Family and Fleet Support Center of Hampton Roads to have representatives to meet the ship at Rota, Spain. These representatives made the "translant" back to CONUS with the ships and offered briefs on all three decks concerning such various topics as: Reunion & Intimacy, Returning to Children, New Parents of Infants, Car Buying, Money Management/ Buyer Beware, Singles Homeward Bound, and Resource Training for Command Leadership. A "New Dad's Shower" was also offered. The MEU Chaplain ensured that the information and schedule of all conferences were widely publicized and urged as many as possible of the MEU Marine and Sailors to attend.

Reports: The MEU Chaplain provided several reports to the II MEF Chaplain on a monthly basis including statistical reports of ministry conducted. The statistical reports were also submitted to the Command Historian for inclusion in the MEU's Command Chronology. The RMT also submitted to the II MEF Chaplain and to the MEU Commander statistics on AMCROSS messages charted on various graphs and reports of status and disposition of each message received. After Action Reports for OPERATION ENDURING FREEDOM, and LF6F 1-02 were submitted to the MEU Commander, II MEF Chaplain, and the Sixth Fleet Chaplain. A copy of the LF6F 1-02 report was sent to the Chaplain of the 22d MEU to help him in his ministry while deployed.

Sixth Fleet and Other Visitations: The Rabbi from the 6th Fleet in Gaeta briefly visited BATAAN while on a port visit at Valletta, Malta. There were not many Jewish personnel identified (only the ship's "Top Doc"-who was not available for Jewish worship services) and so the Chaplain's visit on BATAAN did not involve religious services. He did, however, offer assistance to us and was extremely solicitous to help us in any need that might arise. During "washdown", Naval Station Rota's Chaplains also made ship visitations and welcomed the RMTs warmly offering any kind of assistance that might be needed.

3. LESSONS LEARNED/ RECOMMENDATIONS:

Pre-deployment: The RMT should be fully involved in all of the MEU's pre-deployment activities and exercises. If a new RMT is to be appointed for the MEU, then it should be in place when "workups" begin. And just as it is important for Marines and Sailors to be prepared for deployments, so it is equally necessary for families to be prepared. Insure that as many families of the Marines and Sailors as possible are involved in the pre-deployment activities. The knowledge gained will pay great dividends during the deployment period. Pay careful attention to the Command's Pre-deployment Checklist. Accomplish all taskings on or ahead of schedule.

Translant: Continue to build a strong relationship with ARG Chaplains. Solidify plans for joint ministry when and where possible. Take the time to be more and more present out and around the decks. Continue to learn the living and working spaces of the Marines and Sailors and start regular visitation of these spaces.

Turnovers: Understand that in the future face-to-face turnovers may not happen at turnover times. The incoming Chaplain should be prepared to ask pertinent questions of the outgoing Chaplain when beginning a deployment and have plenty of helpful information available to give to the incoming Chaplain at the end of his deployment.

Portcalls: Understand that the many portcalls enjoyed by past MEUs may be a thing of the past. Be prepared for longer periods underway without port visits, and expect stress to build for the members of the MEU and for the members of the RMT as well. When in port, going on tours is not only a good thing to do, but the experience of tours is a good "jumping off" point for discussions with Marines and Sailors, and will enable the Chaplain to identify with their experiences. It is strongly recommended that the Chaplain take advantage of as many tours as possible as long as ministry on board ship doesn't suffer.

CCPO: It is sincerely hoped that the CCPO program will continue as it gives prospective Chaplains valuable experience. Understand that the program may be "in hiatus" during the period of anti-terrorist operations.

COMRELS: As in the case of port visits, COMRELS may not be as frequent in the near future as they have been in past deployments. Be prepared to work closely with ship's Chaplain, who in turn works closely with husbanding agents in foreign ports. Encourage the participation of MEU Marines and Sailors at every turn.

Ministry: There is no limit to the ministry that can be accomplished on a "float". The Chaplain should be active, pro-active, be seen and be available to any and all personnel at any and all times of the day. The Chaplain should not hesitate to sleep from time to time during the day so that he can deliver ministry during the night hours to those who do not normally have much contact with the Chaplain because of their work schedules. Be sure that before deployment, all supplies needed to provide ministry are on hand. Trying to obtain them while underway is generally a bad idea. It takes too long and the items ordered may never arrive on time to be used effectively.

AMCROSS MESSAGES: Expect a large number of Red Cross Messages to pour in. Conduct good pre-deployment training for Marines, Sailors and their families so that they won't expect that a "return home" will be warranted with every message. Keep close watch on and record every message, and have a special log book to keep records. Present monthly reports to the command.

Operations: Be prepared to participate in all exercises and operations during the deployment. Troop visitation in the field may be difficult at times because of transportation assets. Be prepared to take any and all advantage of any opportunity that presents itself to aid in the delivery of ministry.

Crossdecking For Delivering Ministry: Traveling to other ships to provide ministry is such an important aspect of the Chaplain's job that he should use any available means to accomplish that task. The Chaplain should not hesitate to go "outside" the normal channels (as in the case of using the BLT Air Officer) if it means that ministry will be accomplished.

Awards and Promotions: The Chaplain should encourage the Religious Program Specialist to continually improve in his military proficiencies, and do what he can, ministry not being neglected, to earn his warfare qualifications.

Collateral Duties: Distribution of gift packages and letters may become part of the RMT's job in the future, especially in light of the American public's support of the military. Be prepared to distribute and keep track of packages and letters, and to write "Thank You" letters to the donors.

Billeting: It is desirable that the Chaplain's spaces not be given to visitors. If, however, it is necessary for the spaces to be used by others during any absence of the Chaplain, proper notification should be given in advance so that the Chaplain has the opportunity to secure personal gear.

Careline Updates: The MEU Chaplain should be prepared to write weekly updates to be sent to the "rear" for recording on the MEU Careline. These updates are invaluable for the knowledge and good morale of families left behind, and, as in the case of LF6F 1-02, can prove to be a wonderful public relations tool for the MEU. America wants to know what the young military members are doing.

Return and Reunion Conferences: These conferences have proved not only helpful, but almost essential for the smooth and happy return of the at and deployed Marines and Sailors to their families and loved ones back "home". The MEU Chaplain should work closely with the Ship's Chaplain concerning the arrangement and delivery of these briefs, encourage all Marines and Sailors to attend. It is a wise and fruitful investment of their time.

Reports: Reports are not only useful to the command to know what is going on in the field of ministry, but also to the RMT itself to keep it aware of the progress or needs in various areas. The RMT should be working diligently to see that the various reports are done regularly and completely in accordance with command wishes.

Sixth Fleet and Other Visitations: The Sixth Fleet Chaplains can be an invaluable resource for deployed ARGs. The MEU Chaplain should identify the needs of the Marines and Sailors on the various ARG vessels and enlist the aid of the Sixth Fleet Chaplains when and where necessary. Visits that are non-productive or minimally so should be avoided.

4. SUMMARY:

LF6F 1-02 was a deployment that at times simply "flew by", and at other times seemed to move very slowly. No doubt the extension of a month added a burden of stress to all participants, but nothing that was not handled by the RMTs on ARG shipping. The Religious Ministry Teams of Chaplains and Religious Program Specialists provided timely and effective ministry, whether aboard ship, in "hot" combat areas, or in more quiet locations ashore. The command was fully supportive of all Religious Ministries,

and without that support and encouragement from the command, the ministry would have been little and unproductive. The ship's Command Religious Ministry Department was immensely helpful in delivering ministry to Marines and Sailors deployed. In sum, the

RMTs deployed on LF6F 1-02 are confident that the task of delivering "innovative and life-transforming ministry" to deployed Marines and Sailors was quite successfully accomplished.

J. A. SCORDO
CDR, CHC, USNR
26th MEU Chaplain

Copy to:
SIXTH FLEET, Chaplain
MARFORLANT, Chaplain

A Note from Archbishop O'Brien, DEC/JAN 2001-2002

Dear Joe:

Bravo!

I caught a glimpse of you from Germany on my way home from Bosnia as I watched CNN on Christmas Eve. I then and there thanked the Good Lord for your priestly presence among our men and women in the Afghan wilderness.

What a unique experience Christmas Eve, Christmas Day and, indeed every day there must offer to your priestly call!

We are grateful to you and proud of you, Joe, as we are of every single Marine serving us so willingly and effectively. Please tell them all of our appreciations, support, love and prayers!

In the Lord,

+Edwin F. O'Brien
Archbishop for the Military Services, USA

APPENDIX

Perhaps a more accurate title for this little booklet might have been "Postcards from a Catholic Navy Chaplain". The individual weekly offerings noted here really don't mention much about my ministry as a priest in these deployments. However, in addition to all the port calls and exercises/operations that I experienced, there was a wealth of opportunities for serious and necessary pastoral care. For example, there were countless times when I would be pulled aside on shore or underway for direction in matters that involved family difficulties, marital problems, spiritual matters, or simply for a more "mature" and religious opinion about one thing or another. More than once on our "Beer on the Pier" events I found myself talking with one or several servicemen about some pretty serious religious topics. That's why I always tried to make sure that people knew that the "Padre" was around.

And while we were never allowed to proselytize, many young men and women came to me asking for instructions in the teachings of the Catholic faith. I remember particularly in Afghanistan one day as I was visiting the sick in the medical tents, I paused to pray over a sleeping young Marine. He awoke and began a series of meetings with me discussing his life, family, and religious beliefs. Finally he asked me if he could become a Catholic. When we returned to the ship after the operation ashore, I plugged him into the RCIA (Rite of Christian Initiation for Adults) program that the ship's Catholic Chaplain and I had begun. There were several instances like that one, or where a troop would just show up for the classes and "get in line" so to speak. The end result was many Baptisms, Confirmations, and First Holy Communions while underway.

There were numerous instances when a service man or woman would request the Sacrament of Reconciliation. And often this was not from any fear of imminent danger of an upcoming battle. One day in Kandahar, during a lull in the busy activities of the day, a young Marine came to me for Confession. How wonderful to see the joy and sometimes relief in the faces of those who came to ask for God's forgiveness and mercy! God's grace was simply and clearly at work here, and I had the privilege of doing my part in accomplishing God's will. By the way, I helped that same troop another time in a family death situation. We became friends and are still in contact to this day.

And the celebration of Holy Mass! So much could be said about that. I celebrated Mass just about every day on deployments (most of which were well attended) and in base chapels as well. It's a good thing that I am not a stickler for liturgical niceties, since I found myself offering Mass on tree stumps, boxes of MREs, backs of Humvees, portable tables, ships' library tables and podiums, sometimes in alb and stole, sometimes in camouflage vestments, and sometimes in full Chapel liturgical vestments. You just had to adapt. And, yes, we followed the Liturgical Calendar fairly closely. More than once I celebrated the Sacred Triduum (the three holy days before Easter) while underway. The only thing I really couldn't do was bless the new Easter fire. The most frightening thing a sailor can face is a fire at sea, and I simply could not be (nor was allowed to be) a party to that!

Preaching? Yes, at every Mass. I found that the troops were hungry for the Word of God. How awesome was the chance to help satisfy that hunger. And one of the most memorable times for me was when I stepped foot on the continent of Africa for the first time on St. Dominic's feast day (Aug. 8th). Preaching on yet another continent and on our Patron's feast day—how great is that!

It wasn't too often that I administered the Sacrament of the Sick, but when I did, it was mostly ashore in a hospital in or near a base when a military person had been admitted.

While ashore I celebrated many marriages after having prepared the couple as best I could. And since the military was comprised of mostly younger people, I didn't have many funerals. There were, however, a fair number of "memorial services" that I conducted for units that had lost one of their members, while the funeral proper was conducted at home.

Let me conclude by saying that all of the above was accomplished with the help of my taking care of myself. At the beginning of my military career and during my very first six-month deployment, I recognized the necessity of my taking time to rest, exercise, recreate, do spiritual reading, and pray. When any of these are neglected, ministry suffers. I also found praying the Breviary (Liturgy of the Hours) in stormy seas or in calm to be not only spiritually enriching, but even more importantly (at least for me) very comforting. And the Rosary? How much easier it is to stay close to God with Our Blessed Lady's help. What a fulfilling priestly ministry in the military!

GLOSSARY OF A FEW NAVY/ MARINE CORPS ACRONYMS

The United States Navy and Marine Corps, like any specialized occupation, has its own language. And with the military there are countless acronyms, most of which civilians would not understand. The following is a list of just a few of them to help you understand this (and other military) documents.

ACE . . . . Air Combat Element

AMCROSS . . . . American Red Cross Messages

ARG . . . . Amphibious Readiness Group

BILLET . . . . A job/position or living/sleeping space

BLT . . . . Battalion Landing Team (no, here it doesn't mean that wonderfully delicious sandwich!)

CCPO . . . . Chaplain Candidate Program Officer

CDR . . . . Commander, Navy rank equal to the Army/Marine Corps Lieutenant Colonel

CE . . . . Command Element

CHC . . . . U.S. Navy Chaplain Corps

CISD . . . . Critical Incident Stress Debriefing.

COMRELS . . . . Community Relations Projects

CONUS . . . . loosely, Continental United States

Cover . . . . Navy/Marine Corps for a hat. You are either "covered" or "uncovered". You never have a hat on or off!

CROSS DECK . . . . . going from one ship to another

FARP . . . . Forward Arming and Refueling Point

INCHOP/OUTCHOP . The process of moving to or from the command of any of the Navy's Fleet Areas

LCDR . . . . Lieutenant Commander, Navy rank equal to Army/ Marine Corps Major

LF6F 1-02 . . . . Landing Force Sixth Fleet, First in Fiscal Year 2002

LF6F 3-00 . . . . Landing Force Sixth Fleet, Third in Fiscal Year 2000

MARFORLANT . . . . . Marine Forces Atlantic

MEF . . . . Marine Expeditionary Force

MEU . . . . Marine Expeditionary Unit

MEU SOC . . . . Marine Expeditionary Unit Special Operations Capable

MSSG . . . . MEU Service Support Group

MWR	Morale Welfare and Recreation
NAVCENT	U.S. Naval Forces Central Command
OEF	Operation Enduring Freedom
PHIBGRUP	Amphibious Group
PHIBLEX	Amphibious Landing Exercise
PHIBRON	Amphibious Squadron
PMINT	Amphibious Squadron/Marine Expeditionary Unit Integration
RELIEF	In the military you are not "replaced". The person who takes over your job after you is your "relief".
[ret.]	Retired
RMT	Religious Ministry Team
RP	Religious Program Specialist
[sel.]	Selected for this rank, but not yet promoted
SURFPAC	Naval Surface Forces Pacific
TURNOVER	The process of exchanging information, etc. for deployment units
USNR	United States Naval Reserve
WORKUPS	Multiple training exercises and test that precede any MEU deploymen

PHOTO ALBUM

FORMAL PORTRAITS

Fr. Scordo in Dominican Habit

Fr. Scordo in Military Uniform